NORTHERN
NEW ENGLAND
TRIVIA

NORTHERN
NEW ENGLAND
TRIVIA

Maine, Vermont, and New Hampshire

Compiled by
Daniel and Lisa Ramus

Rutledge Hill Press

513 THIRD AVE., S. NASHVILLE, TENNESSEE 37210

Published by Rutledge Hill Press, Inc., 513 Third Avenue South, Nashville, Tennessee 37210

Typography by Bailey Typography, Inc.

Library of Congress Cataloging-in-Publication Data

Ramus, Daniel, 1960-
    Northern New England trivia : Maine, Vermont, and New Hampshire / compiled by Daniel and Lisa Ramus.
        p. cm.
    ISBN 1-55853-066-5
    1. New England—Miscellanea.   2. Maine—Miscellanea. 3. New Hampshire—Miscellanea. 4. Vermont—Miscellanea.
    5. Questions and answers.   I. Ramus, Lisa, 1958-   .   II. Title.
    F4.5.R36   1990   90-32567
    974—dc20   CIP

Printed in the United States of America
1 2 3 4 5 6 7 8 — 95 94 93 92 91 90

PREFACE

Known for its outstanding natural beauty and relaxed lifestyle, Northern New England has always been a playground. The activities available—skiing, hunting, fishing, boating, and hiking—are more diverse than anywhere else in our country.

Come join us for a Penobscot Bay sail on a schooner, topped off with an island lobster bake. Enjoy a day of crosscountry skiing from one mountain inn to another along a wintry stream. Or just travel the Vermont country roads, dotted with dairy farms and white steepled churches.

Northern New England—see how much you know about this beautiful part of our country!

Good Luck!

—Daniel and Lisa Ramus

To our son Sam—a native Mainer
with a true Yankee Spirit!

TABLE OF CONTENTS

GEOGRAPHY

C H A P T E R O N E

Q. Campobello, a Canadian island off the coast of Maine, was the summer home of what former president of the United States?

A. Franklin D. Roosevelt.

———◆———

Q. What was the first alpine slide in the nation?

A. Bromley's.

———◆———

Q. On what bay does Portland, Maine, lie?

A. Casco.

———◆———

Q. What state contains the only railroad covered bridge in the country still in use?

A. Vermont.

———◆———

Q. What New Hampshire national forest contains 730,000 acres?

A. White Mountain.

Q. In what New Hampshire city is Prescott Park situated?

A. Portsmouth.

———◆———

Q. In what Maine town are Frye Boot, Hathaway Shirt, and L. L. Bean stores situated?

A. Freeport.

———◆———

Q. What is the theme at Clark's Trading Post, an amusement park in Lincoln, New Hampshire?

A. Victoriana.

———◆———

Q. The Palabra Museum, Boothbay Harbor, Maine, is reputed to have the world's largest collection of bottles shaped like whom?

A. Moses.

———◆———

Q. In what mountain range is the Mount Washington Hotel situated?

A. The Presidential Range.

———◆———

Q. How many sanctuaries does the Audubon Society of New Hampshire manage?

A. Eleven.

———◆———

Q. What is the sixth largest lake in the United States?

A. Lake Champlain.

Q. What state park is the largest in New Hampshire?

A. Pisquah.

———◆———

Q. In what month do the blueberry festivals usually begin in Maine?

A. August.

———◆———

Q. What noted American architect designed the Maine State Capitol Building (1829)?

A. Charles Bulfinch.

———◆———

Q. The city of Bangor, Maine, is at the head of what major river?

A. The Penobscot.

———◆———

Q. Where in New York does the Burlington, Vermont, ferry land?

A. Port Kent.

———◆———

Q. Is the Mount Washington Observatory a public or private operation?

A. Private.

———◆———

Q. What is the name of the road going to the top of Mount Washington?

A. Auto Road.

Q. In what New Hampshire town is Wildcat Mountain?

A. Jackson.

Q. What river divides southern Maine and New Hampshire?

A. The Piscataqua.

Q. Where is the international airport in Vermont?

A. Burlington.

Q. In what town is the Maine Maritime Museum found?

A. Bath.

Q. What is the only national park in New England?

A. Acadia, Maine.

Q. What living museum in New Gloucester, Maine, features the wooden furniture and implements of America's oldest religious community?

A. Shaker Museum.

Q. Where is the end of the Maine Turnpike, which begins in York?

A. Augusta.

Q. What Maine city is often referred to as the "Queen City"?

A. Bangor.

———◆———

Q. What state is considered the toothpick capital of the world?

A. Maine.

———◆———

Q. In colonial times, what northern boundary was marked by Endicott Rock at Weirs Beach, New Hampshire?

A. The northern boundary of Massachusetts.

———◆———

Q. Built in 1969, where is the newest covered bridge in Vermont?

A. Woodstock.

———◆———

Q. How many ferry crossings are there on Lake Champlain between Vermont and New York?

A. Four.

———◆———

Q. What state park, encompassing 250,000 acres, did Gov. Percival Baxter give to the state of Maine?

A. Baxter.

———◆———

Q. On what lake is Weirs Beach?

A. Lake Winnipesaukee.

Q. What is the capital of Maine?

A. Augusta.

———◆———

Q. What is the biggest city in Vermont?

A. Burlington.

———◆———

Q. Aroostook County in Maine is larger than what two New England states combined?

A. Rhode Island and Connecticut.

———◆———

Q. What river forms the famous Quechee Gorge in Vermont?

A. The Ottauquechee.

———◆———

Q. What New Hampshire organization is one of the oldest statewide handicrafts associations in the country?

A. The League of New Hampshire Craftsmen.

———◆———

Q. What is the theme of New Hampshire's amusement park, Six Gun City?

A. The Wild West.

———◆———

Q. Route 4 in Vermont crosses what 165-foot deep gorge?

A. Quechee Gorge.

Q. To what household items is the museum in Thorndike, Maine, devoted?

A. Stoves (The Bryant Stove Museum).

———◆———

Q. In the early 1900s, what Manchester, New Hampshire, textile plant was the largest in the world?

A. The Amoskeag Mill Yard.

———◆———

Q. What geometric shape is the Portland Observatory, the last remaining signal tower from the 1800s on the Atlantic coast?

A. Octagonal.

———◆———

Q. What city has the largest population in the three northern New England states?

A. Manchester, New Hampshire.

———◆———

Q. What town is at the highest altitude in New England?

A. Dublin, New Hampshire.

———◆———

Q. What is the nation's smallest capital city?

A. Montpelier, Vermont.

———◆———

Q. Where is the New England Dragway?

A. Epping, New Hampshire.

Q. What kind of horses are found at the Anheuser-Busch Brewery?

A. Clydesdales.

Q. The largest city in New Hampshire was named after what city in England?

A. Manchester.

Q. Berthed in Castine, Maine, the ship *State of Maine* is used for what purpose?

A. Training for the Maine Maritime Academy.

Q. How is Harriet Beecher Stowe's home in Brunswick, Maine, presently used?

A. As an inn.

Q. What city in New Hampshire is the only city in the state with an Atlantic coastline?

A. Portsmouth.

Q. What can be seen posted on the trees along the Robert Frost National Recreational Trail?

A. Frost's poems, mounted on plaques.

Q. Fort Kent was built as a defense against what nation?

A. Canada.

Q. Where in Maine is the annual Bean Pole Bean Festival held?

A. Oxford Hills.

———◆———

Q. What shape is the Brookline, Vermont, brick schoolhouse, which was built in 1822?

A. Round.

———◆———

Q. What is Maine's oldest public art museum?

A. Portland Museum of Art.

———◆———

Q. What trading post printed T-shirts saying "L. L. Who?"

A. Kittery Trading Post.

———◆———

Q. What is the highest point on the east coast?

A. Cadillac Mountain in Maine.

———◆———

Q. Cannon Mountain in Lincoln, New Hampshire, is part of what state park?

A. Franconia Notch State Park.

———◆———

Q. In what city do ferries depart from the Customs House wharf?

A. Portland, Maine.

Q. What U.S. president is buried in Plymouth, Vermont?

A. Calvin Coolidge.

———◆———

Q. What is the name of Franklin Pierce's Concord, New Hampshire, home that is now an historic site?

A. Pierce Manse.

———◆———

Q. How many people can travel together in a gondola at Wildcat Mountain?

A. Two.

———◆———

Q. The New Hampshire Highland Games, the largest gathering of Scots in New England, are held at what place?

A. Loon Mountain.

———◆———

Q. Who owns the Grand Isle in Lake Champlain?

A. Vermont.

———◆———

Q. What is the specialty product of Perham's Maine Mineral Store in West Paris?

A. Maine gems and rocks.

———◆———

Q. In what state is the Robert Hull Fleming Museum the primary fine arts museum?

A. Vermont.

Q. What ornate house in Kennebunk, Maine, is named after a cake?

A. The Wedding Cake House.

———◆———

Q. On what New England mountain was the first aerial tramway built in 1938?

A. Cannon.

———◆———

Q. What can be seen at Annalee's Museum in Meredith, New Hampshire?

A. Dolls.

———◆———

Q. Neal Dow, whose memorial is in Portland, Maine, was a general during what war?

A. The Civil War.

———◆———

Q. In 1955, the S.S. *Ticonderoga* was moved from Lake Champlain to what Vermont city?

A. Shelburne.

———◆———

Q. For what sign do campers look in Vermont?

A. VAPCOO (Vermont Association of Private Campground Owners and Operators).

———◆———

Q. What publication does the DeLorme Publishing Company of Freeport, Maine, print for many states?

A. A state atlas and gazeteer.

Q. The northern end of what national trail is at Mount Katahdin, Maine?

A. The Appalachian National Scenic Trail.

———◆———

Q. What great face is the symbol of the state of New Hampshire?

A. The Old Man of the Mountains.

———◆———

Q. For what sign do campers look in Maine?

A. MECOA (Maine Campground Owners Association).

———◆———

Q. What New Hampshire dam is the location for New England's largest hydroelectric plant?

A. Moore.

———◆———

Q. Fort Halifax, the oldest blockhouse in the United States, monitored what river?

A. The Kennebec.

———◆———

Q. What Air Force base is near the Portsmouth Naval Shipyard?

A. Pease.

———◆———

Q. What are the two major north-south interstate highways in Vermont?

A. Routes 91 and 89.

Q. What are the three largest cities in New Hampshire?

A. Manchester, Nashua, and Concord.

———◆———

Q. What is the motto of Vermont?

A. "Freedom and Unity."

———◆———

Q. What famous animal is depicted by a statue in Marine Park, Rockport, Maine?

A. Andre the Seal.

———◆———

Q. What is the steepest grade on the Mount Washington Cog Railway called?

A. Jacob's Ladder.

———◆———

Q. In what New Hampshire town did Gov. John Wentworth build the first known summer home?

A. Wolfeboro.

———◆———

Q. What ninety-mile waterway and preserve in upstate Maine is popular for canoe trips?

A. Allagash Wilderness Waterway.

———◆———

Q. What New England state has the widest east-west measurement?

A. Maine.

Q. During what season is the Maple Syrup Festival held in Vermont?

A. Early spring.

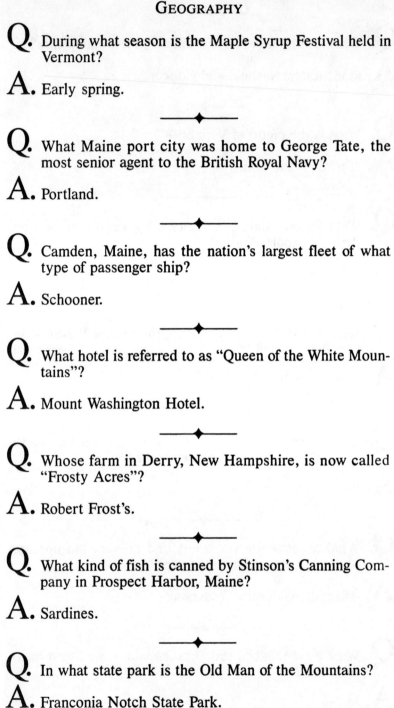

Q. What Maine port city was home to George Tate, the most senior agent to the British Royal Navy?

A. Portland.

Q. Camden, Maine, has the nation's largest fleet of what type of passenger ship?

A. Schooner.

Q. What hotel is referred to as "Queen of the White Mountains"?

A. Mount Washington Hotel.

Q. Whose farm in Derry, New Hampshire, is now called "Frosty Acres"?

A. Robert Frost's.

Q. What kind of fish is canned by Stinson's Canning Company in Prospect Harbor, Maine?

A. Sardines.

Q. In what state park is the Old Man of the Mountains?

A. Franconia Notch State Park.

Q. The estate museum of what famous Revolutionary War general is in Thomaston, Maine?

A. General Henry Knox.

———◆———

Q. Where on the coast is Maine's largest campground, with about 600 sites?

A. Old Orchard Beach.

———◆———

Q. Whose home was converted for use as the Knox and Lincoln Railroad Depot, the oldest depot in America?

A. General Henry Knox's.

———◆———

Q. After Alaska, what state has the greatest tide range in the United States?

A. Maine.

———◆———

Q. What river flows under the covered bridge that connects Windsor, Vermont, and Cornish, New Hampshire?

A. The Connecticut.

———◆———

Q. What New Hampshire mountain has the state's longest aerial ride?

A. Loon.

———◆———

Q. What ethnic heritage is celebrated during the Midsummer Festival in New Sweden, Maine?

A. Scandinavian

Q. At what time do state-operated parks open in Vermont?

A. 10:00 A.M.

Q. How many lakes comprise Maine's Belgrade Lakes region?

A. Seven.

Q. What cow spent seventy-six days with a Vermont moose in 1985?

A. Jessica.

Q. What is the name of Amtrak's train that goes through Vermont?

A. The Montrealer.

Q. What Maine city was once the largest ship mast port in the British Empire?

A. Portland.

Q. What are listed in Vermont's brochure, "The Red Clover Trail"?

A. Farms that welcome visitors.

Q. What explorer's home can be visited in Harpswell (Eagle Island), Maine?

A. Admiral Robert E. Peary's.

Q. What Maine college hosts the Maine Festival each year?

A. Bowdoin College, in Brunswick.

———◆———

Q. What is the largest of the Penobscot Bay Islands?

A. Vinalhaven.

———◆———

Q. Where is the lowest elevation in the state of Vermont?

A. Lake Champlain.

———◆———

Q. How much was the original toll on the footbridge at Waterville, Maine, one of the few remaining in the United States?

A. Two cents.

———◆———

Q. Fort Popham in Phippsburg, Maine, guarded the mouth of what river during the Revolutionary War?

A. The Kennebec.

———◆———

Q. To what island does the Acadia Trail, Route 3, take visitors?

A. Mount Desert.

———◆———

Q. What are the two national forests in New England?

A. White Mountain and Green Mountain.

Q. What powers the trains at Boothbay Railway Village in Maine?

A. Steam.

———◆———

Q. In what town is the New England Ski Museum situated?

A. Franconia, New Hampshire.

———◆———

Q. What is the first daily event at the Maine Lobster Festival, held annually in Rockland?

A. A pancake breakfast.

———◆———

Q. On what bay is Rockland, Maine?

A. Penobscot.

———◆———

Q. Where can you ride to the highest point reached by aerial lift in New England?

A. Killington Peak (4,241 feet).

———◆———

Q. More than half of New Hampshire's residents live within thirty-five minutes of what city?

A. Manchester.

———◆———

Q. Machias, Maine, was the scene of the first naval battle of what war?

A. The Revolutionary War.

Q. Where was the first licensed merry-go-round in the United States?

A. Old Orchard Beach, Maine.

———◆———

Q. Through what state do the Lamoille, Missisquoi, Battenkill, and Otter Creek rivers run?

A. Vermont.

———◆———

Q. What is Maine's only international border city?

A. Calais.

———◆———

Q. What museum preserves a record of the lumber industry in northern Maine?

A. The Lumberman's Museum.

———◆———

Q. In what national forest is the Robert Frost National Recreational Trail?

A. Green Mountain.

———◆———

Q. Where is one of the largest walk-through spook houses?

A. Old Orchard Beach Amusement Park, Maine.

———◆———

Q. What is the oldest United States naval shipyard?

A. Portsmouth Naval Shipyard.

Q. Acadia National Park, known for its lush vegetation and rare wildlife, contains what Maine city?

A. Bar Harbor.

Q. The name of what mountain was changed to Mount Eisenhower to honor the thirty-fourth president?

A. Mount Pleasant.

Q. In what month is the Maine Potato Blossom Festival held?

A. July (usually the third week, when the potatoes blossom).

Q. In what New England town does the famous Route 1 end?

A. Fort Kent, Maine.

Q. August 16 is a Vermont state holiday commemorating what battle?

A. The Battle of Bennington.

Q. In what town is the natural sand "Desert of Maine" to be found?

A. Freeport, Maine.

Q. Button Bay State Park, in Vermont, is on the shore of what body of water?

A. Lake Champlain.

Q. What Maine sporting goods store is open 365 days a year, 24 hours a day?

A. L. L. Bean.

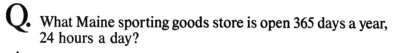

Q. What is the second smallest state capital in the country?

A. Augusta, Maine.

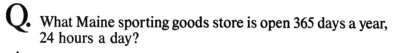

Q. What is the nation's first state craft center?

A. The Vermont Craft Center, Frog Hollow, in Middlebury, Vermont.

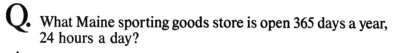

Q. What brewery is in Merrimack, New Hampshire?

A. Anheuser-Busch, Inc.

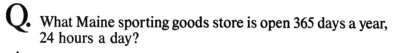

Q. How many Native Americans live on Maine's three federal Indian reservations?

A. 2,500.

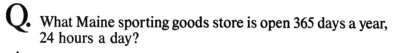

Q. What Maine summer resort do Canadians visit more than any in their own country?

A. Old Orchard Beach.

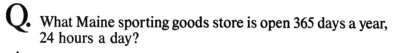

Q. What famous Old Orchard Beach pier was destroyed in the storm of February 1978?

A. Ocean Pier.

Q. What is the name of the famous excursion boat on Lake Winnipesaukee?

A. *Mount Washington.*

———◆———

Q. Where is New Hampshire's only state-owned airport?

A. Rochester.

———◆———

Q. How many toll roads are there in Maine?

A. One.

———◆———

Q. How many American youth hostels are there in Vermont?

A. Eight.

———◆———

Q. What Maine island is the only national monument in New England?

A. Saint Croix.

———◆———

Q. What Vermont lodge is named after a famous Austrian family?

A. Trapp Family Lodge.

———◆———

Q. How old is the "sunken forest" of Rye, New Hampshire?

A. 3,500 years old.

Q. What is known as the "Coney Island of Maine"?

A. Old Orchard Beach.

Q. Where can you find a casino in New Hampshire?

A. Hampton Beach (Club Casino).

Q. What New Hampshire town is believed to have the widest main street in the United States?

A. Keene (172 feet).

Q. How many people can travel together in each gondola at Loon Mountain?

A. Four.

Q. What wood carving, probably the largest of its type in the world, is found in Skowhegan, Maine?

A. A wooden Indian.

Q. Who attacks each train at Clark's Trading Post in Lincoln, New Hampshire?

A. Backwoodsmen.

Q. What Maine town was once called Eden because of its beauty?

A. Bar Harbor.

Q. What Maine company, named for the town where it is situated, makes world-famous canoes?

A. The Old Town Company.

Q. What is the oldest covered bridge in Vermont?

A. The Pulp Mill Bridge.

Q. What is one of the biggest flea markets in the northeast?

A. Newfane Flea Market, Vermont.

Q. How long is the toll road to the top of Mount Washington?

A. Eight miles.

Q. What can be seen at The Game Preserve in Petersborough, New Hampshire?

A. The nation's second largest collection of board and card games.

Q. How many people can ride together in the Jay Peak Tramway at the Jay Peak ski area?

A. Sixty.

Q. What products can visitors watch being made at Tom's of Maine, Inc., in Kennebunk, Maine?

A. Toothpaste, shampoo, and deodorant.

Q. What famous resort is on the shore of Lake Gloriette in Dixville Notch, New Hampshire?

A. The Balsams.

———◆———

Q. What 200-ton capacity machine, found in Maine, is the only one of its kind in the Western Hemisphere?

A. The Whirley Crane.

———◆———

Q. What college is in Bennington, Vermont?

A. Bennington College.

———◆———

Q. What amusement park is in Salem, New Hampshire?

A. Canobie Lake Park.

———◆———

Q. What is Maine's southernmost and oldest county?

A. York.

———◆———

Q. Keag Village, Maine, is the center of what town?

A. South Thomaston.

———◆———

Q. What Vermont city has the largest concentration of precision tool manufacturing plants in the nation?

A. Springfield.

Q. What county in western Maine forms most of the United States' border between Canada and Maine?

A. Oxford.

Q. What Maine lake is in Johnson Memorial Park?

A. Chickawaukie Lake.

Q. What Maine city is the largest in area, but with a population of only 5,200?

A. Ellsworth.

Q. A thousand-foot-long heap of shells was left by the Indians on what Maine island?

A. Pond Island.

Q. Where is the Vermont State Fair held?

A. Rutland.

Q. What town is the site of Maine's largest annual fall agricultural fair?

A. Fryeburg.

Q. What town was the site of New Hampshire's only WWII prisoner of war camp?

A. Stark.

Q. What national park is in Vermont?

A. There is no national park in Vermont.

———◆———

Q. In 1895, the State of Maine Building was moved to Poland Spring, Maine, from what international exposition?

A. Chicago's.

———◆———

Q. What valley contains 750,000 acres of national forest?

A. Mount Washington Valley.

———◆———

Q. What type of equipment is manufactured in North Berwick, Maine, at the Hussy Corporation, founded in 1835?

A. Farm equipment.

———◆———

Q. What Maine city once had the names Casco and Falmouth?

A. Portland.

———◆———

Q. The New England Culinary Institute is in what Vermont city?

A. Montpelier.

———◆———

Q. What kind of pine tree, abundant in Maine, has given that state its nickname?

A. The Eastern white pine.

Q. In classical mythology, Ceres, whose statue is atop Vermont's capitol building, was goddess of what endeavor?

A. Roman goddess of agriculture.

Q. What Maine museum contains a boatbuilding school?

A. The Bath Marine Museum.

Q. What powers the streetcars at the Seashore Trolley Museum in Kennebunkport, Maine?

A. Electricity.

Q. What is the highest mountain in Baxter State Park in Maine?

A. Mount Katahdin.

Q. Near what kind of geographical feature is a Class A camping facility in Vermont always found?

A. A recreational body of water.

Q. At what Vermont museum can you find a display of Grandma Moses' paintings and the largest collection of Bennington pottery?

A. Bennington Museum.

Q. What is Maine's largest inland body of water?

A. Moosehead Lake.

Q. What is the number of the highway, called "the scenic route," along the Maine coast?

A. Route 1.

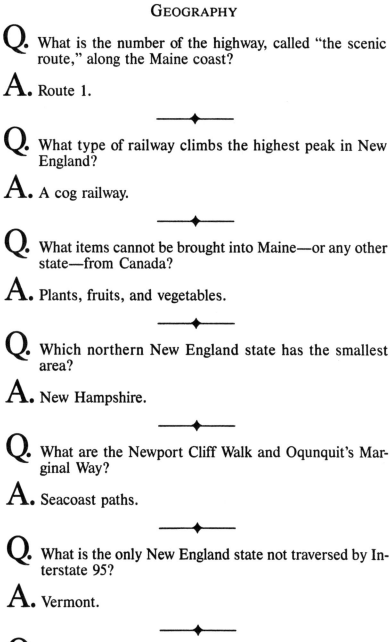

Q. What type of railway climbs the highest peak in New England?

A. A cog railway.

Q. What items cannot be brought into Maine—or any other state—from Canada?

A. Plants, fruits, and vegetables.

Q. Which northern New England state has the smallest area?

A. New Hampshire.

Q. What are the Newport Cliff Walk and Oqunquit's Marginal Way?

A. Seacoast paths.

Q. What is the only New England state not traversed by Interstate 95?

A. Vermont.

Q. How many New England states are bordered by the St. Lawrence River?

A. None.

Q. What two Canadian provinces border northern New England?

A. New Brunswick and Quebec.

———◆———

Q. Cushing, Maine, stretches for ten miles along the west bank of what river?

A. St. George River.

———◆———

Q. How many covered bridges still exist in Maine?

A. Nine.

———◆———

Q. The lighthouse at West Quoddy in Lubec, Maine, marks what geographically important point in the United States?

A. The easternmost point.

———◆———

Q. The longest covered bridge in the nation crosses the border of what two states?

A. New Hampshire and Vermont.

———◆———

Q. What is the second most frequently visited national park in the United States?

A. Acadia.

———◆———

Q. Of the nine Isles of Shoals, five belong to Maine, with the other four belonging to what state?

A. New Hampshire.

Q. What are southern Maine's "twin cities"?

A. Saco and Biddeford.

———◆———

Q. What state has produced more wooden sailing ships than any other?

A. Maine.

———◆———

Q. Maine's border with Canada extends for how many miles?

A. 610.

———◆———

Q. What Maine city has more forts in its immediate vicinity than any other community?

A. Portland.

———◆———

Q. Many of the signs in Old Orchard Beach, Maine, are printed in what two languages?

A. French and English.

———◆———

Q. What is New Hampshire's nickname?

A. The Granite State.

———◆———

Q. What two northern New England states have approximately the same greatest east-west measurement of ninety miles?

A. New Hampshire and Vermont.

Q. What three towns does Sunapee Lake lie within?

A. Sunapee, Newbury, and New London.

———◆———

Q. The wild Ammonoosuc River runs between what two cities, one on Route 3 and the other on Route 302?

A. North Woodstock and Bath.

———◆———

Q. Which northern New England state has the least population density per square mile?

A. Maine.

———◆———

Q. How many counties are there in New Hampshire?
A. Ten.

———◆———

Q. What are the four Connecticut lakes?

A. First Lake, Second Lake, Third Lake, and Lake Francis.

———◆———

Q. What stream joins the Connecticut River at West Claremont?

A. The Sugar River.

———◆———

Q. What river enters the Connecticut River at Hinsdale?
A. Ashuelot.

Q. What is the longest stream in New Hampshire?

A. Otter Creek.

———◆———

Q. What island marks the eastern side of Penobscot Bay?

A. Isle au Haut.

———◆———

Q. What is the smallest inhabited island of the Penobscot Bay Islands?

A. Monhegan.

———◆———

Q. What is Maine's third largest lake?

A. Chesuncook.

———◆———

Q. In what direction is Little Sebago Lake from Sebago Lake?

A. East.

———◆———

Q. On what route between Naples and Harrison can one see the "Million Dollar View" of Long Lake with the White Mountains in the background?

A. Route 35.

———◆———

Q. What are the two largest lakes in Naples, Maine?

A. Long Lake and Brandy Pond.

Q. What town is eight miles north of Rockland, Maine, on Route 1?

A. Camden.

———◆———

Q. Matinicus, Maine, is the largest of two groups of islands at the entrance to what bay?

A. Penobscot.

———◆———

Q. How far is Vinalhaven off the coast of Rockland in Penobscot Bay?

A. Ten miles.

———◆———

Q. In what county is Rockland, Maine?

A. Knox.

———◆———

Q. What is the easternmost city in the United States?

A. Eastport, Maine.

———◆———

Q. How many counties are there in Maine?

A. Sixteen.

———◆———

Q. What county in Maine has the greatest area?

A. Aroostook.

Q. The twin cities of Lewiston and Auburn lie on opposite sides of what major river?

A. The Androscoggin.

———◆———

Q. What Maine town lies precisely halfway between the Equator and the North Pole?

A. Great Pond.

———◆———

Q. What does the symbol of a spinning wheel represent when used on Vermont's official state map?

A. Crafts/antiques.

———◆———

Q. What type of vessel is the U.S.S *Albacore,* which is in a museum in Portsmouth, New Hampshire?

A. A submarine.

———◆———

Q. What is the Green Mountain Flyer, found in Bellows Falls, Vermont?

A. A train.

———◆———

Q. What sports championships are held in Jamaica, Vermont, each year?

A. Canoe and kayak.

———◆———

Q. What Vermont town was the birthplace of Calvin Coolidge?

A. Plymouth Notch.

Q. Where is Ethan Allen's hometown?

A. Sunderland, Vermont.

Q. Addison, Vermont, is home to what historic museum?

A. The DAR (Daughters of the American Revolution) Museum.

Q. What is special about the 294-foot bridge in Brookfield, Vermont?

A. It is floating.

Q. Where is the New England Maple Museum?

A. Pittsford, Vermont.

Q. What are the Mount Jasper Caves in Berlin, New Hampshire?

A. Old Indian mines.

Q. What town is the home of Mount Chocorua?

A. Chocorua, New Hampshire.

Q. What trail leads to the Bridal Falls in Franconia?

A. Coppermine Trail.

Q. What is in Page's Garage in Haverhill, New Hampshire?

A. Early Fords (Model A's).

———◆———

Q. What is the distance visible from the top of Mount Washington?

A. 150 miles, under best conditions.

———◆———

Q. What New Hampshire town was called both Madbury and Adams before its name was changed to honor a president?

A. Jackson.

———◆———

Q. Where is Moosilauke Mountain?

A. Warren, New Hampshire.

———◆———

Q. What is the largest festival held in Portsmouth, New Hampshire?

A. Market Square Day.

———◆———

Q. Where was the summer home of Woodrow Wilson?

A. Cornish, New Hampshire.

———◆———

Q. In what town's Science Center can patrons view an eagle at close range?

A. Holderness, New Hampshire.

Q. General John Stark, whose home is in Manchester, New Hampshire, fought in what war?

A. The Revolutionary War.

HISTORY

Q. In 1778, Thomas Chittenden was governor of what state?

A. Vermont.

———◆———

Q. What was Vermont's original name?

A. New Connecticut.

———◆———

Q. Where was Chester A. Arthur, twenty-first president of the United States, born?

A. Fairfield, Vermont.

———◆———

Q. In what war did Franklin Pierce enlist as a private and rise to brigadier general?

A. Mexican War.

———◆———

Q. The flags of what four nations have flown over Fort George in Castine, Maine?

A. France, England, Holland, and the United States.

Q. According to Maine legend, Mollyocket, "the great Indian doctress," saved the life of what future vice president?

A. Hannibal Hamlin.

———◆———

Q. What Vermont native assisted President Eisenhower but resigned after being criticized for accepting gifts?

A. Sherman Adams.

———◆———

Q. What 1905 treaty ended the war between Russia and Japan?

A. The Treaty of Portsmouth (New Hampshire).

———◆———

Q. In 1912, what young girls' organization was founded on Lake Sebago, Maine?

A. Campfire Girls.

———◆———

Q. In 1944, what New Hampshire resort was the site of the United Nations Monetary and Financial Conference?

A. Bretton Woods.

———◆———

Q. What town, settled in the early 1600s, is the oldest community in Maine?

A. Kittery.

———◆———

Q. What was the occupation of Maine native Dixie Bull?

A. Piracy.

Q. What state was called "the Switzerland of North America" by nineteenth-century historian Lord Bryce?

A. Vermont.

———◆———

Q. What naval yard built the sloop *Kearsage*, which defeated the Confederate raider *Alabama* in a memorable Civil War battle?

A. Portsmouth Naval Shipyard.

———◆———

Q. The large sphinx statue in the Mount Auburn Cemetery commemorates the dead of what war?

A. The Civil War.

———◆———

Q. What Vermont town claims to be the "Birthplace of Vermont"?

A. Windsor.

———◆———

Q. What president was the first Democrat ever to win Vermont?

A. Lyndon B. Johnson.

———◆———

Q. What college was founded in 1769 for the "education and religious training of Indians, English youth and others?"

A. Dartmouth College (Hanover, New Hampshire).

———◆———

Q. Where does the all-male Ethan Allen Club meet?

A. Burlington, Vermont.

Q. What state was the first in the nation to prohibit slavery?

A. Vermont.

Q. In 1851, Portland, Maine, passed the "Maine Law," eliminating what product from the city?

A. Liquor.

Q. During what war did the only battle fought in Vermont take place at the Hubbardton Battlefield?

A. The American Revolution.

Q. What was the name of the first U.S. battleship, launched in 1890?

A. U.S.S. *Maine*.

Q. Who won the New Hampshire Democratic presidential primary in 1988?

A. Michael Dukakis.

Q. What state is the birthplace of Joseph Smith, founder of the Mormon Church?

A. Vermont.

Q. What was named after Dorothy Ann Durgun, the first eldress at a Shaker village in New Hampshire?

A. The "Dorothy cloake" (a cape).

Q. In 1790, what was issued, for the first time, to Samuel Hopkins of Vermont?

A. A United States patent.

———◆———

Q. What publication was banned by the FBI during part of 1944?

A. *Old Farmer's Almanac.*

———◆———

Q. Franklin Pierce's wife was the daughter of the president of what New England college?

A. Bowdoin College (Brunswick, Maine).

———◆———

Q. What event broke off the wedding between Lucy Hale of Dover, New Hampshire, and John Wilkes Booth?

A. The assassination of Abraham Lincoln.

———◆———

Q. Calvin Coolidge became president after the death of what president?

A. Warren G. Harding.

———◆———

Q. Under the banner of what political party did Calvin Coolidge run for president in 1924?

A. Republican.

———◆———

Q. What state was admitted as the fourteenth state?

A. Vermont.

Q. What were the specialty products of the Shaker Sabbath-day Lake Village in Maine?

A. Wooden products.

———◆———

Q. John Langdon of New Hampshire declined an offer to become vice president to what president?

A. James Madison.

———◆———

Q. What two New England states did not vote for Franklin D. Roosevelt in any of his four elections?

A. Maine and Vermont.

———◆———

Q. New Hampshire's Jeremiah Jones Colbath, vice president under Ulysses S. Grant, was known by what other name?

A. Henry Wilson.

———◆———

Q. What state was the first to include universal manhood suffrage in its constitution?

A. Vermont.

———◆———

Q. Where did the northernmost land actions of the Civil War take place?

A. St. Albans, Vermont (a raid by Confederate soldiers).

———◆———

Q. Who had the nicknames "Handsome Frank" and "Purse"?

A. Franklin Pierce.

Q. At the Battle of Bennington, how many points were on the stars on the Continental army flag?

A. Seven.

———◆———

Q. Where is Crown Point, which was captured by Ethan Allen in 1775?

A. Southern Lake Champlain.

———◆———

Q. To what New Hampshire statesman is attributed the quotation "Liberty and Union, now and forever, one and inseparable"?

A. Daniel Webster.

———◆———

Q. In 1866, what destroyed fifteen hundred buildings in Portland, Maine?

A. Fire.

———◆———

Q. Bangor, Maine, is reputed to be the birthplace of what legendary lumberman?

A. Paul Bunyan.

———◆———

Q. Vermont's Thaddeus Stevens played a major role in what period of U.S. history?

A. Reconstruction in the South following the Civil War.

———◆———

Q. Nelson Aldrich Rockefeller was vice president for what president?

A. Gerald R. Ford.

Q. In 1972, to whom did Sen. Edmund Muskie of Maine lose the Democratic presidential nomination?

A. George McGovern.

———◆———

Q. What state was the first in the country to outlaw the manufacture and sale of alcoholic beverages?

A. Maine (in 1851).

———◆———

Q. General Henry Knox was secretary of war for what U.S. president?

A. George Washington.

———◆———

Q. Edmund Muskie of Maine was secretary of state for what U.S. president?

A. Jimmy Carter.

———◆———

Q. What state was almost named New Somerset?

A. Maine.

———◆———

Q. What U.S. president was born in Hillsboro, New Hampshire?

A. Franklin Pierce.

———◆———

Q. For what nation did Samuel de Champlain claim Lake Champlain?

A. France.

Q. What New Hampshire mill once produced 2,700 miles of cloth a week?

A. Amoskeag Mills.

———◆———

Q. What state was the birthplace of Calvin Coolidge?

A. Vermont.

———◆———

Q. What kind of wood was used to build one of the nation's oldest log cabins, the Hyde Log Cabin in Montpelier, Vermont?

A. Cedar.

———◆———

Q. The longest covered bridge in the United States, built in 1886, connects what two towns?

A. Windsor, Vermont, and Cornish, New Hampshire.

———◆———

Q. What northern New Englander became the only president to be sworn in at his home by his father?

A. Calvin Coolidge.

———◆———

Q. Of what stone are the walls of the Vermont state house made?

A. Vermont granite.

———◆———

Q. In what year did the Portsmouth Naval Shipyard build thirty-two submarines?

A. 1944.

Q. Why was the Webster-Ashburton Treaty of 1842 important to the United States?

A. It settled the border dispute establishing the line between Canada and Maine.

------◆------

Q. Who used Smuggler's Notch in Vermont during the War of 1812?

A. Smugglers bringing goods from Canada to Boston.

------◆------

Q. What was Vermont's first permanent white settlement?

A. Fort Dummer (1724).

------◆------

Q. What major firm did Eben Jordan create?

A. Jordan Marsh Company.

------◆------

Q. What section of Portsmouth, New Hampshire, got its name from wild berries found by its settlers?

A. Strawbery Banke.

------◆------

Q. Built in Vergennes, Vermont, what was the name of Thomas MacDonough's flagship?

A. *Saratoga.*

------◆------

Q. In 1776, a New Hampshire town was first to honor President Washington in what special way?

A. The town was named Washington.

Q. What may be the nation's oldest tax-supported free public library, founded in 1833?

A. The library in Peterborough, New Hampshire.

———◆———

Q. What famous poet is buried in the Old Burying Ground in Bennington, Vermont?

A. Robert Frost.

———◆———

Q. In 1964, what state instituted the first legal U.S. lottery since the 1890s?

A. New Hampshire.

———◆———

Q. What kind of boat is the *Ticonderoga,* now moored in Vermont?

A. A sidewheeler.

———◆———

Q. What was the name of the group of Vermont settlers formed in 1770 and led by Ethan Allen?

A. The Green Mountain Boys.

———◆———

Q. In what cemetery are the gravestones of Winslow Homer, H. W. Longfellow, and Henry Cabot Lodge?

A. Mount Auburn Cemetery.

———◆———

Q. What is the oldest Roman Catholic church surviving in New England?

A. St. Patrick's (New Castle, Maine).

Q. From what New England college did Henry W. Long-fellow, Nathaniel Hawthorne, and Franklin Pierce all graduate in 1825?

A. Bowdoin College (Brunswick, Maine).

Q. What was the first name of Calvin Coolidge's wife?

A. Grace.

Q. Nelson A. Rockefeller was the only one of John D. Rockefeller's five sons to be born in what Maine town?

A. Bar Harbor.

Q. What Maine town staged a "tea party" similar to the more famous one in Boston?

A. York.

Q. In 1846, New Hampshire senator John Parker Hale secured the abolition of what practice in the United States Navy?

A. Flogging.

Q. For what war did the C. F. Hathaway Company make uniforms?

A. The Civil War.

Q. Who was nicknamed "Black Dan"?

A. Daniel Webster.

Q. In 1856, who refused his party's nomination to run for a second term as President?

A. Franklin Pierce.

Q. What two New England colonies provided the English with masts for their ships?

A. Maine and New Hampshire.

Q. What state of the original thirteen was the first to form its own government?

A. New Hampshire.

Q. What was the first capital city of Maine?

A. Portland.

Q. What woman from Bethel, Maine, was a leader in the temperance movement in Oxford County?

A. Agnes Straw Mason.

Q. What Vermonter is regarded as the father of modern, progressive education in America?

A. John Dewey.

Q. What United States government position did New Hampshire's John Pickering hold when he was impeached?

A. Federal district judge.

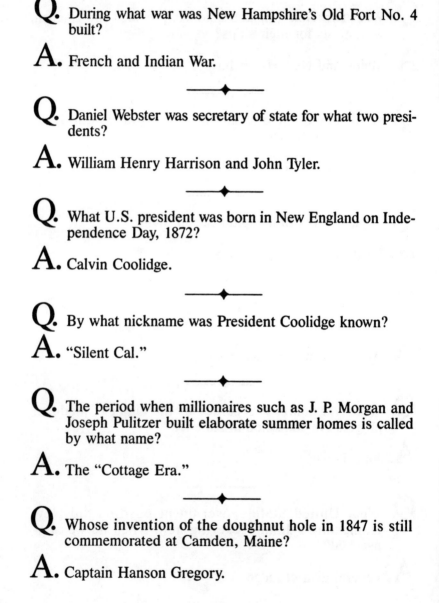

Q. Who probably were the first white people to visit the Maine coast?

A. The Vikings, about 1000 A.D.

Q. During what war was New Hampshire's Old Fort No. 4 built?

A. French and Indian War.

Q. Daniel Webster was secretary of state for what two presidents?

A. William Henry Harrison and John Tyler.

Q. What U.S. president was born in New England on Independence Day, 1872?

A. Calvin Coolidge.

Q. By what nickname was President Coolidge known?

A. "Silent Cal."

Q. The period when millionaires such as J. P. Morgan and Joseph Pulitzer built elaborate summer homes is called by what name?

A. The "Cottage Era."

Q. Whose invention of the doughnut hole in 1847 is still commemorated at Camden, Maine?

A. Captain Hanson Gregory.

Q. In 1934, the U.S. Supreme Court finally determined the boundary between what two New England states?

A. New Hampshire and Vermont.

———◆———

Q. What president was instrumental in arranging the signing of the important Treaty of Portsmouth, following the war between Russia and Japan?

A. Theodore Roosevelt.

———◆———

Q. In 1948, what woman from Maine became the first Republican woman to serve in the United States Senate?

A. Margaret Chase Smith.

———◆———

Q. What two New England states were not included in the original thirteen?

A. Maine and Vermont.

———◆———

Q. In April 1865, General Joshua L. Chamberlain of Maine was appointed by Ulysses S. Grant to receive the surrender of what general?

A. Robert E. Lee.

———◆———

Q. What western city was founded by Vermont's Brigham Young?

A. Salt Lake City, Utah.

———◆———

Q. Who was the first president of the United States from Vermont?

A. Chester A. Arthur.

Q. What New England college did Daniel Webster attend?

A. Dartmouth College (Hanover, New Hampshire).

◆

Q. The king of what country tried, but failed, to settle a boundary dispute between Maine and New Brunswick in 1831?

A. The Netherlands.

◆

Q. What New Englander argued that states cannot tax a federal agency because the power to tax involves the "power to destroy"?

A. Daniel Webster.

◆

Q. In 1874, the Canterbury Shaker village in New Hampshire produced between three and four thousand pounds of what product?

A. Maple sugar.

◆

Q. What was the last New England state to enter the Union?

A. Maine (1820).

◆

Q. Neal Dow, born in Portland, Maine, was what party's candidate for U.S. president in 1880?

A. Prohibition Party.

◆

Q. When Massachusetts bought Maine in 1677 from the heirs of Ferdinando Gorges, how much did Massachusetts pay?

A. Six thousand dollars.

Q. What coach, built in Concord, New Hampshire, hauled passengers throughout America?

A. The Concord coach.

———◆———

Q. What town was the capital of New Hampshire during the Revolutionary War?

A. Exeter.

———◆———

Q. When the clipper ship *Red Jacket* set a speed record in 1854 for crossing the Atlantic Ocean, what was its sailing time?

A. Just over thirteen days.

———◆———

Q. What large oil company did John D. Rockefeller found?

A. Standard Oil.

———◆———

Q. On what lake did Thomas MacDonough meet the British in battle on September 11, 1814?

A. Lake Champlain.

———◆———

Q. Whose headquarters did Henry Longfellow's father-in-law buy, to give the property to Longfellow for a wedding present?

A. George Washington's.

———◆———

Q. During Prohibition times, what lake was the scene of many skirmishes between law enforcement agents and bootleggers?

A. Lake Champlain.

Q. What New England capital has the nation's oldest original capitol building still in use?

A. Concord, New Hampshire.

———◆———

Q. Vermont's Green Mountain Boys threw out speculators holding land titles from what state?

A. New York.

———◆———

Q. What Maine railroad connecting Bethel and Portland was completed in 1851?

A. Atlantic and St. Lawrence Railway.

———◆———

Q. Where is the Jonathan Fisher Memorial?

A. Blue Hill, Maine.

———◆———

Q. What organization, the largest of its kind in the nation, is known by the acronym SPNEA?

A. Society for the Preservation of New England Antiquities.

———◆———

Q. Who was the first woman to make a solo flight—which originated in Maine—over the Atlantic Ocean?

A. Amelia Earhart.

———◆———

Q. From what state did Maine separate in 1820?

A. Massachusetts.

Q. From whom did the early New England settlers learn to make maple syrup?

A. The Indians.

———◆———

Q. What kind of wood is used for the splints on the traditional New Hampshire Shaker basket?

A. Ash.

———◆———

Q. What heavenly body guided runaway slaves through northern New England to their freedom in Canada?

A. The North Star.

———◆———

Q. What name was given to the United States flag by northern New England sea captain William Driver in 1831?

A. Old Glory.

———◆———

Q. What famous admiral owned Eagle Island in Casco Bay?

A. Admiral Robert E. Peary.

———◆———

Q. What city boasts the only shipyard in America where large wooden sailing vessels are still constructed?

A. Bath, Maine.

———◆———

Q. During which century were most of the towns on the southern coast of Maine settled?

A. Seventeenth.

Q. What community was the first in Maine to establish zoning laws?

A. York Harbor.

Q. Who was the commander of the privateer *Ranger*, built in Kittery, Maine?

A. John Paul Jones.

Q. When was the country's first five-masted schooner built in Waldoboro, Maine?

A. 1856.

Q. In 1937, what famous gangster was shot on the streets of Bangor, Maine?

A. Al Brady.

Q. What New Hampshire community was the third oldest English settlement on the Atlantic seaboard?

A. Portsmouth.

Q. In 1723, what pirate is said to have left his wife on the Isles of Shoals?

A. Blackbeard.

Q. Sangerville, Maine, is the only small town in the nation that has had two native sons receive what honor?

A. They were knighted by royalty.

Q. What state was the ninth to enter the Union?

A. New Hampshire.

———◆———

Q. New Hampshire was controlled by what colony from 1641 until it was made a separate royal colony in 1680?

A. Massachusetts.

———◆———

Q. What is the origin of the term *Down East*, first used by sailors?

A. Coastal winds made the trip from Boston to Maine easy or "down hill."

———◆———

Q. What were the hardwood pegs called that were used to fasten the timbers on old boats?

A. Treenails (or "trunnels").

———◆———

Q. In 1604, who explored the area around St. Anthony's Monastery in Kennebunk?

A. Samuel de Champlain.

———◆———

Q. Who was president when St. Patrick's Church in New Castle, Maine, was constructed?

A. Thomas Jefferson.

———◆———

Q. What was the name of the first submarine built in the Portsmouth Naval Shipyard?

A. *L 8.*

Q. Who was the first Roman Catholic governor of Maine?

A. Edward Kavanagh.

———◆———

Q. To what town was the Hodge School moved from Washington, Maine?

A. Union, Maine.

———◆———

Q. Who served two terms as Maine's U.S. Congressman, 1833–1837?

A. Dr. Moses Mason.

———◆———

Q. What year was the Portsmouth Naval Shipyard established?

A. 1800.

———◆———

Q. The Nordica Homestead in Farmington, Maine, was the birthplace of what world-famous singer?

A. Lillian Nordica.

———◆———

Q. Where is the memorial to Maine's Neal Dow?

A. Congress Street, Portland.

———◆———

Q. Where in Maine is the historic home of writer Sarah Orne Jewett?

A. South Berwick.

Q. What is Maine's second largest lake?

A. Sebago Lake.

Q. What is the name of the only covered bridge in historic Cumberland County, Maine?

A. Babb's Covered Bridge.

Q. In what year did the Cumberland and Oxford Canal close?

A. 1870.

Q. How many training, research, and pleasure vessels does the Maine Maritime Academy have?

A. Ninety.

Q. What town in Maine is known as the "Lobster Capital of the World"?

A. Rockland.

Q. Out of twenty-seven hand-operated locks built in the 1830s to make navigation possible from Harrison to the ocean at Portland, how many remain?

A. One.

Q. Sir William Pepperell of Kittery Point, Maine, was commander-in-chief of what Revolutionary War expedition?

A. Louisburg.

Q. What river in Maine is listed in the *Guinness Book of Records* as the world's shortest river?

A. Chute's River.

———◆———

Q. How many paper mills were built in Maine between 1730 and 1890?

A. Twenty-five.

———◆———

Q. What grist mill in Lebanon, Maine, is believed to be one of the oldest original wooden grist mills in the country?

A. The Olde Grist Mill.

———◆———

Q. What New England state has the fewest members in the United States House of Representatives?

A. Vermont (one).

———◆———

Q. What U.S. president was referred to as "Loose Lips"?

A. Calvin Coolidge.

———◆———

Q. How much land is occupied by Maine's three Indian reservations?

A. 245,424 acres.

———◆———

Q. Who wrote, "There is no right to strike against the public safety by anybody, anywhere, anytime"?

A. Calvin Coolidge.

Q. New Hampshirite George H. Whipple shared a 1934 Nobel Prize in medicine for what discovery?

A. The use of liver to treat anemia.

———◆———

Q. What member of the Rockefeller family owned 11,000 acres of Mount Desert Island, Maine?

A. John D. Rockefeller, Jr.

———◆———

Q. In what state were the alarm clock, the horse blanket, and the internal combustion engine invented?

A. New Hampshire.

———◆———

Q. In 1849, what kind of saw did Lemuel Hedge of Windsor, Vermont, invent?

A. Band saw.

———◆———

Q. What national political event occurs first in New Hampshire, every four years?

A. The presidential primary.

———◆———

Q. How did Horace Wells of Vermont use laughing gas for the first time?

A. As an anesthetic for pulling teeth.

———◆———

Q. What state in the nation has the most members in its House of Representatives?

A. New Hampshire (400).

Q. Hiram Maxim of Maine was knighted by Queen Victoria for what invention?

A. The machine gun.

Q. What was Vermont's governmental status for the fourteen years prior to statehood?

A. Independent republic.

Q. What happened on July 8, 1777, at a tavern in Windsor, Vermont?

A. The constitution of the Republic of Vermont was adopted.

Q. What royal governor of New Hampshire established grants for the three million acres west of the Connecticut River?

A. Benning Wentworth.

Q. What were the "Hampshire Grants" (circa 1770)?

A. New York's claims to Vermont soil.

Q. After what state's constitution was Vermont's constitution patterned?

A. Pennsylvania's.

Q. Who founded Vermont's Shelburne Museum in 1947?

A. Mr. and Mrs. Watson Webb.

Q. What Vermont senator wrote the act establishing land-grant colleges?

A. Justin Smith Morrill.

———◆———

Q. The brass cannon at the Vermont State House was captured from Hessian soldiers during what war?

A. The American Revolution.

———◆———

Q. Who opened a school for women in 1814 on the site of Middlebury College?

A. Emma Willard.

———◆———

Q. How long was Edmund Muskie U.S. secretary of state?

A. Eight months.

———◆———

Q. What Skowhegan, Maine, native was the first woman nominated for the United States presidency by a major party?

A. Margaret Chase Smith.

———◆———

Q. What land company planted the seed that later became the state of Vermont?

A. Onion River Land Company.

———◆———

Q. What state published a pamphlet stating it was "designed by the creator for the playground of the continent"?

A. Vermont.

Q. To what group did Remember Baker of Arlington, Vermont, belong?

A. The Green Mountain Boys.

———◆———

Q. Where was Daniel Webster born?

A. Franklin, New Hampshire.

———◆———

Q. What Massachusetts governor signed Endicott Rock in Weirs Beach, New Hampshire?

A. John Endicott.

———◆———

Q. Where was Horace Greeley born?

A. Amherst, New Hampshire.

———◆———

Q. What famous Christian Scientist was born in Bow, New Hampshire?

A. Mary Baker Eddy.

———◆———

Q. Where was the first permanent settlement in New Hampshire?

A. Dover (1632).

———◆———

Q. Where are Friendship sloops built?

A. Friendship, Maine.

ARTS & LITERATURE

CHAPTER THREE

Q. What is the only law school in Maine?

A. University of Southern Maine School of Law.

———◆———

Q. What was the setting for Harriet Beecher Stowe's novel *The Pearls of Orr's Island?*

A. Orr's Island, Maine.

———◆———

Q. What Exeter, New Hampshire, native wrote *The World According to Garp?*

A. John Irving.

———◆———

Q. What U.S. president offered poet Edwin Arlington Robinson, who was born in Head Tide, Maine, a clerkship in the New York Custom House?

A. Theodore Roosevelt.

———◆———

Q. *Yankee Magazine* claims all rights reserved for the peacetime use of what name?

A. Yank.

Q. What famous children's poem was written by Sarah Josepha Hale of Newport, New Hampshire?

A. "Mary Had a Little Lamb."

———◆———

Q. What did novelist Booth Tarkington use as his workshop while he lived in Kennebunk, Maine?

A. His beached schooner.

———◆———

Q. On what island did artist Rockwell Kent settle in 1905?

A. Monhegan Island.

———◆———

Q. In what New Hampshire town is the *Old Farmer's Almanac* published?

A. Dublin.

———◆———

Q. What famous poet often wrote under "The Whittier Pine" in Centre Harbor, New Hampshire?

A. John Greenleaf Whittier.

———◆———

Q. What song associated with singer Rudy Vallee refers to his native state?

A. "Maine Stein Song."

———◆———

Q. What husband-wife team (he was born in Fairfield, Maine) described raising twelve children in their best-selling *Cheaper By the Dozen?*

A. Frank and Lillian Gilbreth.

Q. What New England poet is the only American whose bust is in the Poets Corner of Westminster Abbey, London, England?

A. Henry Wadsworth Longfellow.

———◆———

Q. At what college is the Hood Museum of Art located?

A. Dartmouth College (Hanover, New Hampshire).

———◆———

Q. What magazine, purchased by Cyrus H. K. Curtis of Maine, became one of the most successful periodicals ever published?

A. *The Saturday Evening Post.*

———◆———

Q. Who was the mean overseer and slave driver in *Uncle Tom's Cabin,* written by Harriet Beecher Stowe?

A. Simon Legree.

———◆———

Q. What was the name of the first long poem, written at age nineteen, by Maine-born poet Edna St. Vincent Millay?

A. "Renascence."

———◆———

Q. Who is the Maine-born author of *Pet Sematary?*

A. Stephen King.

———◆———

Q. The writing talent of Helen Gurley Brown, who was born in Portland, Maine, was discovered when her husband found what?

A. Love letters to a former lover.

Q. What author, born in South Berwick, Maine, wrote *Country of the Pointed Firs?*

A. Sarah Orne Jewett.

———◆———

Q. Who painted *View of Bluehill* in 1824?

A. Jonathan Fisher.

———◆———

Q. A men's tricycle, jointed dolls, and a device for shelling boiled eggs were invented in what Vermont town?

A. Springfield.

———◆———

Q. What does the 1909 painting *Right and Left* by Winslow Homer show?

A. Ducks brought down by two shots from a double-barreled shotgun.

———◆———

Q. Wells Woods Inn in Plainfield, New Hampshire, was the home of what famous painter?

A. Maxfield Parrish.

———◆———

Q. What Maine author wrote *Northwest Passage, Arundel, Rabble in Arms, Boon Island,* and *Oliver Wiswell?*

A. Kenneth Roberts.

———◆———

Q. What poet taught at Pinkerton Academy in Derby, New Hampshire, and at Amherst College in Massachusetts?

A. Robert Frost.

Q. What major magazine often used Norman Rockwell paintings on its front cover?

A. *The Saturday Evening Post.*

———◆———

Q. What Vermont city has the oldest municipal musical group in the United States?

A. Rutland.

———◆———

Q. In what Maine city did Henry Wadsworth Longfellow grow up?

A. Portland.

———◆———

Q. The Walker Art Building on what Maine college campus has a Winslow Homer collection?

A. Bowdoin College.

———◆———

Q. What Kenneth Roberts novel was written about an island off the coast of his Kennebunkport home?

A. *Boon Island.*

———◆———

Q. What religion did Mary Baker Eddy of New Hampshire found?

A. Christian Science.

———◆———

Q. What was the first established public university (1791) in the United States?

A. University of Vermont.

Q. For what kind of art was Augustus Saint-Gaudens of Cornish, New Hampshire, famous?

A. Sculptures.

———◆———

Q. What artist used two hundred of his Vermont neighbors and friends to create his "everyday life" paintings?

A. Norman Rockwell.

———◆———

Q. What are the Passamaquoddy, the Penobscot, and the Maliseet?

A. Indian tribes.

———◆———

Q. At what New Hampshire college is the Hopkins Center for the Performing Arts?

A. Dartmouth.

———◆———

Q. Who wrote "Fight fire with fire and craft with craft"?

A. Henry Wadsworth Longfellow.

———◆———

Q. What Carolyn Chute bestseller was about poverty in Maine?

A. *The Beans of Egypt, Maine.*

———◆———

Q. What major American artist is renowned for his realistic pictures of people and places in rural Maine?

A. Andrew Wyeth.

Q. How many paintings are attributed to Norman Rockwell?

A. About 5,000.

Q. What Disney character was designed by Maurice Day in his Maine studio?

A. Bambi.

Q. Who co-authored *The Double Man* with Maine state senator William Cohen?

A. Senator Gary Hart.

Q. How many times did Maine poet Edwin Arlington Robinson win a Pulitzer Prize?

A. Three.

Q. In what did sculptor John Jaley Bellamy specialize?

A. Eagles.

Q. Joy Farm, near Silver Lake in New Hampshire, was the summer home of what famous poet?

A. e. e. cummings.

Q. What New England magazine, established in 1935, publishes a swapper's column each month?

A. *Yankee Magazine.*

Q. What artist of *Next Wave* "discovered" Maine in the early 1900s?

A. Frederick Judd Waugh.

———◆———

Q. What is the name of the "Magazine of Maine," published in Camden?

A. *Down East.*

———◆———

Q. What artist spent summers in Cornish, New Hampshire, and painted covers for *Life* and *Collier's* magazines?

A. Maxfield Parrish.

———◆———

Q. What is the oldest continuously published periodical in the United States?

A. *Old Farmer's Almanac.*

———◆———

Q. What was the name of Hiawatha's wife in Longfellow's poem *Hiawatha*?

A. Minnehaha.

———◆———

Q. What poem won Edwin Arlington Robinson the Pulitzer Prize in 1924?

A. *The Man Who Died Twice.*

———◆———

Q. What 1981 Oscar-winning movie was filmed in New Hampshire?

A. *On Golden Pond.*

Q. What New England writer won the Pulitzer Prize four times for his poetry?

A. Robert Frost.

———◆———

Q. What man is known as the "Father of Maine"?

A. Sir Ferdinando Gorges.

———◆———

Q. Who wrote *The Jungle Book* while living in a bungalow in Vermont?

A. Rudyard Kipling.

———◆———

Q. Robb and Trix Sagendorph are the founders of what New England magazine?

A. *Yankee Magazine.*

———◆———

Q. Admiral Robert S. Peary, a graduate of Bowdoin College, is known for what exploratory achievement?

A. He was the first man to reach the North Pole.

———◆———

Q. What color is associated with Dartmouth College?

A. Green.

———◆———

Q. Dartmouth College used an optical scanning computer to read what great poem by Dante Alighieri?

A. *The Divine Comedy.*

Q. Where is the New England magazine *Country Journal* published?

A. Brattleboro, Vermont.

◆

Q. What was the setting of *On Golden Pond* that was filmed in New Hampshire?

A. Belgrade Lakes in Maine.

◆

Q. What talent did New Hampshire's Maxfield Parrish display in *The Saturday Evening Post?*

A. Illustrator.

◆

Q. Who wrote the poem "What Lips My Lips Have Kissed"?

A. Edna St. Vincent Millay.

◆

Q. Mistie-Mokwa and Mishe-Nahma were characters in what epic poem?

A. *Hiawatha.*

◆

Q. What famous poet wrote a poem about the arsenal in Springfield, Vermont?

A. Longfellow.

◆

Q. Longfellow's poem *The Courtship of Miles Standish* is about what group of people?

A. The Pilgrims.

ARTS AND LITERATURE

Q. What famous artist had a home in Prouts Neck, Maine?

A. Winslow Homer.

———◆———

Q. In the late 1800s, what artist painted Cushing's Island in Portland Harbor?

A. Alfred Thompson Bricher.

———◆———

Q. The epitaph on whose tombstone reads, "I had a lover's quarrel with life"?

A. Robert Frost.

———◆———

Q. Where was Horace Greeley born?

A. Amherst, New Hampshire.

———◆———

Q. What major newspaper was founded and edited by Horace Greeley?

A. The New York *Tribune*.

———◆———

Q. What is the current name of Waterville College in Maine?

A. Colby College.

———◆———

Q. What building houses the art museum of Bowdoin College, Brunswick?

A. Walker Art Building.

Q. In what book by Kenneth Roberts does the French and Indian War volunteer military group Roger's Rangers appear?

A. *Northwest Passage.*

———◆———

Q. What college gave an honorary degree to author Sarah Orne Jewett, the first woman to receive such a degree from the college?

A. Bowdoin.

———◆———

Q. "Into each life some rain must fall" is a line from what Longfellow poem?

A. "The Rainy Day."

———◆———

Q. In what subject did Vermont-born Rudy Vallee major at Yale?

A. Spanish.

———◆———

Q. What is New Hampshire's largest private prep school?

A. Phillips Exeter Academy.

———◆———

Q. What university is in Northfield, Vermont?

A. Norwich.

———◆———

Q. Who wrote: "Two roads diverged in a wood, and I—/I took the one less traveled by,/ And that has made all the difference"?

A. Robert Frost.

Q. While in New Hampshire, Thorton Wilder wrote what Pulitzer Prize winning play?

A. *Our Town.*

Q. What famous poet was said to have been inspired by the Portland Head Lighthouse when he wrote the poem, "The Lighthouse"?

A. Longfellow.

Q. What border in northern Maine did Longfellow immortalize in his poem *Evangeline*?

A. St. John River.

Q. George Curtis's *The Storm Within* is a sculpture made of what materials?

A. The remains of a fish, a lobster pot, and a net.

Q. What church is associated with St. Paul's private school in Concord, New Hampshire?

A. Episcopal.

Q. The Southwest Harbor Maine Museum contains more than 200 carvings of what kind of animals by Wendell Gilley?

A. Birds.

Q. Who paints under the name of Zsissly?

A. Malvin Albright.

Q. James Elliott of West Bath, Maine, uses water colors to paint what subjects?

A. Waves, rocks, and trees.

———◆———

Q. In what television series did University of Vermont graduate Jon Cypher portray Chief Daniels?

A. "Hill Street Blues."

———◆———

Q. What sculptor, who spent his summers in Cornish, New Hampshire, created the Sherman statue near Central Park in New York?

A. Augustus Saint-Gaudens.

———◆———

Q. What computer language was invented by John Kemeny and Thomas Kurtz at Dartmouth College?

A. BASIC.

———◆———

Q. What movie starred Linda Lavin, a Portland, Maine, native, along with Joan Rivers and some famous puppets?

A. *The Muppets Take Manhattan.*

———◆———

Q. Henry Varnum Poor came to Maine to join the faculty of what newly formed school?

A. Skowhegan School of Painting and Sculpture.

———◆———

Q. What author, philosopher, and prototype nonviolent activist wrote a journal of his visit to *The Maine Woods?*

A. Henry David Thoreau.

Q. The monthly magazine *Profile* contains articles written about what state?

A. New Hampshire.

———◆———

Q. What is the highest academic degree conferred by Middlebury College in Vermont?

A. Doctorate.

———◆———

Q. Harriet Beecher Stowe's novel, *Life Among the Lowly,* is better known by what title?

A. *Uncle Tom's Cabin.*

———◆———

Q. What does Dahlou Ipcar, daughter of Marguerite Zorach, usually paint?

A. Animals.

———◆———

Q. In what town did Norman Rockwell spend fourteen years creating most of his work?

A. Arlington, Vermont.

———◆———

Q. In 1836, for whom did Charles Codman paint *Old State House?*

A. Gov. Robert P. Dunlap of Brunswick, Maine.

———◆———

Q. Charles Gordon Cutler's *Maine Lobsterman* is a carving of what material?

A. Granite.

Q. What 1900 Winslow Homer painting has the words, "Painted fifteen minutes after sunset—not one minute before"?

A. *West Point, Prouts Neck.*

———◆———

Q. Why is a hole punched in the corner of each issue of the *Old Farmer's Almanac*?

A. To hang it up, especially in the outhouse.

———◆———

Q. What is *The Spirit of the Sea,* William Zorach's gift to Maine, unveiled in Bath in August 1962?

A. A fountain.

———◆———

Q. What movie was filmed in Cape Neddick and Cape Porpoise, Maine, in the summer of 1989?

A. *Bed and Breakfast.*

———◆———

Q. What famous artist, who lived his last twenty-seven years in Prouts Neck, Maine, covered the Civil War for *Harper's Weekly?*

A. Winslow Homer.

———◆———

Q. What 1987 film, starring Bette Davis, was shot on Hope Island in Casco Bay, Maine?

A. *The Whales of August.*

———◆———

Q. Where in Maine is the U.S. Motherhouse of the Lithuanian Franciscans?

A. Kennebunkport.

Q. What university has a 124-acre seaside campus in Maine and offers a program with a doctor of osteopathy degree?

A. The University of New England.

———◆———

Q. The clipper ship *Nightingale,* built in Eliot, Maine, in 1851, was named for what famous singer?

A. Jenny Lind.

———◆———

Q. What New England state has the lowest average public school teacher salaries?

A. Vermont.

———◆———

Q. What year was Edwin Arlington Robinson's *The Torrent and the Night Before* privately published?

A. 1897.

———◆———

Q. What was the title of Edwin A. Robinson's first volume of poetry?

A. *The Children of the Night.*

———◆———

Q. What sculptor produced *Tuna* in Cape Neddick, Maine?

A. Robert Laurent.

———◆———

Q. In 1923, who wrote the highly respected *Body of This Death?*

A. Louise Bogan.

Q. What three plays of Edna St. Vincent Millay were published in 1921?

A. *Two Slatterns and a King, The Lamp and the Bell,* and *Aria Da Capo.*

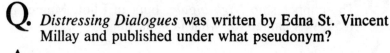

Q. *Distressing Dialogues* was written by Edna St. Vincent Millay and published under what pseudonym?

A. Nancy Boyd.

Q. Where was Louise Bogan born?

A. Livermore Falls, Maine.

Q. Who designed Grotto of Our Lady of Lourdes and Chapel of the Stations of the Cross in Kennebunkport, Maine?

A. James Mulokas.

Q. What is the style of architecture of St. Patrick's Church in New Castle, Maine?

A. Early Federal.

Q. Val McGann does paintings primarily of Ireland and what state?

A. Maine.

Q. Born in Shamut, Maine, who is referred to as Maine's "Renaissance Man"?

A. Leonard Craig.

Q. Where in Vermont is New England's most important collection of American folk art?

A. Shelburne Museum.

———◆———

Q. Who is both the founder and director of Monadnock Music?

A. James Bolle

———◆———

Q. Co-founder of the *Maine Times,* who began his newspaper career in Maine over thirty years ago?

A. John Cole.

———◆———

Q. Who was executive director of The Society for the Preservation of New England Antiquities for twenty-eight years?

A. Abbot Cummings.

———◆———

Q. For what audience does New England author Tomie dePaola write books?

A. Children.

———◆———

Q. What New Hampshire actor toured the country portraying George Bernard Shaw in a one man show?

A. Bramwell Fletcher.

———◆———

Q. R. Buckminster Fuller, summer resident of Bear Island, Maine, is known for what invention?

A. The geodesic dome.

Q. What eighty-year resident of Maine was awarded the U.S. Medal of Freedom by Ronald Reagan?

A. R. Buckminster Fuller.

———◆———

Q. What Keene, New Hampshire, native wrote *The Dogs of March?*

A. Ernest Herbert.

———◆———

Q. Ernest Herbert writes a weekly column for what New England magazine?

A. *Boston Sunday Globe Magazine.*

———◆———

Q. What New Hampshirite wrote *The Natural Foods Cookbook?*

A. Beatrice Trum Hunter.

———◆———

Q. What was the profession of Deering, New Hampshire, resident Lotte Jacobi?

A. Photographer.

———◆———

Q. Up to how many novels has Stephen King had on the best-seller list at one time?

A. Three.

———◆———

Q. New Hampshire resident Maxine Cumin received the Pulitzer Prize for what book of poetry?

A. *Up Country.*

Q. Authors Scott and Helen Nearing of Harborside, Maine, write books on what topic?

A. Nature/back to the land.

———◆———

Q. New Hampshire politician Rob Trowbridge was also president of what New England publishing company?

A. Yankee.

———◆———

Q. Artist Jamie Wyeth spends half the year on what Maine Island?

A. Monhegan.

———◆———

Q. Sinclair Lewis's novel, *It Can't Happen Here,* is set in what state?

A. Vermont.

———◆———

Q. What were the first two institutions of higher education in Vermont?

A. University of Vermont (1791) and Middlebury College (1800).

———◆———

Q. What Maine town is regarded as the first place that Mary Baker Eddy practiced the Christian Science faith?

A. Warren.

———◆———

Q. What was the first art museum in Maine to be accredited by The American Association of Museums?

A. Farnsworth Museum, Rockland.

Q. The Shore Village Museum in Rockland, Maine, houses the country's largest collection of what type of artifacts?

A. Coast Guard/lighthouse.

Q. Bernard Langlois of Maine is well known for animal sculptures of what material?

A. Rough wood.

Q. Where is the Barker Library, which contains many rare manuscripts?

A. Dartmouth College.

Q. Where was nineteenth-century editor Sarah Josepha Hale born?

A. Newport, New Hampshire.

Q. Known as one of the best small museums in the country, what Manchester gallery houses many American decorative artworks?

A. The Currier Gallery.

Q. In what New Hampshire town has *The Old Homestead* been performed for nearly fifty years?

A. Swanzey.

Q. What New Hampshire seacoast town is home to a great children's museum?

A. Portsmouth.

Q. Robert Frost taught at what academy in Derry, New Hampshire?

A. Pinkerton.

———◆———

Q. Poet Celia Thaxter lived on what New Hampshire island?

A. Appledore Island, Isles of Shoals.

———◆———

Q. What teacher-poet-essayist-novelist-biographer born in Brunswick, Maine, won the 1936 Pulitzer Prize for poetry?

A. Robert P. Tristram Coffin.

———◆———

Q. A rock formation on New Hampshire's Profile, or Cannon, Mountain was made famous in the short story "The Great Stone Face" by what New England author?

A. Nathaniel Hawthorne.

———◆———

Q. What children's book by Rachel Field describes experiences of a French servant girl in Maine?

A. *Calico Bush.*

———◆———

Q. What Vermont-born writer describes events similar to his youth in his novel *A Day No Pigs Would Die?*

A. Robert N. Peck.

———◆———

Q. What Amherst, New Hampshire, native first said, "Go West, young man"?

A. Horace Greeley.

Q. *Godey's Lady Book,* which helped shape the tastes and thoughts of nineteenth-century American women, was edited by what native of Newport, New Hampshire?

A. Sarah Josepha Hale.

———————◆———————

Q. What freed black slave in the eighteenth century bequeathed to Jaffrey, New Hampshire, money that to this day provides prizes for high school students in debate and oratory?

A. Amos Fortune *(Amos Fortune, Free Man).*

SPORTS & LEISURE

C H A P T E R   F O U R

Q. What type of lift was invented and first installed at the Pico ski area in 1940?

A. T-bar.

———◆———

Q. What trail goes over Mount Mansfield in Vermont?

A. The Long Trail.

———◆———

Q. What New Hampshire ski area displays an original EB and LRR locomotive?

A. Loon Mountain.

———◆———

Q. What Vermont group is known by the initials GMC?

A. The Green Mountain Club.

———◆———

Q. The world's longest snowmobile journey, which ended in Lubec, Maine, started in what state?

A. Washington.

Q. The best whitewater rafting in Maine starts at the beginning of what month?

A. May.

———◆———

Q. In what state is the world championship Holy Mackerel Fishing Tournament held?

A. Maine.

———◆———

Q. What kind of vessel was the *Double Eagle II*, the first of its kind to travel across the Atlantic?

A. Hot air balloon.

———◆———

Q. What is the name of the Maine Phillies' hometown ballpark?

A. The Ballpark.

———◆———

Q. At what Scarborough, Maine, track did harness racing take place?

A. Scarborough Downs.

———◆———

Q. The West River in Vermont has been the site of what sport's regional and national championships?

A. Whitewater kayaking.

———◆———

Q. At what Olympic games did Andrea Mead Lawrence of Rutland, Vermont, ski the Olympic flame into the stadium?

A. Squaw Valley, California.

Q. What ski area is in the same town as the Mount Washington Hotel?

A. Bretton Wood.

———◆———

Q. What college can be seen from the Hanover, New Hampshire, portion of the Appalachian Trail?

A. Dartmouth.

———◆———

Q. Canoes of what brand are manufactured in Waitsfield, Vermont?

A. Mad River.

———◆———

Q. In what state is the only New England Outward Bound school?

A. Maine.

———◆———

Q. What kind of surgery did Joan Benoit have seventeen days before the Olympic trials?

A. Knee surgery.

———◆———

Q. How many AMC Huts are there along the Appalachian Trail in the White Mountains of New Hampshire?

A. Eight.

———◆———

Q. What is the only state park in Maine that accepts reservations?

A. Baxter.

Q. Down what famous ravine can one ski in the Mount Washington Valley?

A. Tuckermans Ravine.

———◆———

Q. In 1952, Andrea Mead Lawrence of Vermont won two U.S. gold medals in what Olympic event?

A. Skiing (slalom and giant slalom).

———◆———

Q. About what subject did Jim Fixx write?

A. Running.

———◆———

Q. In what state is Squaw Ski Mountain?

A. Maine.

———◆———

Q. What is unique about the Nansen Ski Club of Berlin, New Hampshire, founded in 1872?

A. It was the first ski club in the United States.

———◆———

Q. Bud Leavitt was the first man from Maine welcomed into what international hall of fame?

A. Fishing.

———◆———

Q. What recreational event takes place each August in Castine, Maine?

A. The Retired Skippers Race.

Q. What sport is played at the World Mud Bowl each year in North Conway, New Hampshire?

A. Touch mud football.

———◆———

Q. Starting in 1985, at what ski area is the Volvo International Tennis Tournament held?

A. Stratton Mountain.

———◆———

Q. What organization uses the Leon L. Bean Mountain Center in Bethel, Maine?

A. Outward Bound.

———◆———

Q. Where is the baseball park of the Maine Phillies?

A. Old Orchard Beach.

———◆———

Q. Along what highway is the Loon Mountain ski area situated?

A. Kancamagus.

———◆———

Q. The PROFILE was the first U.S. company to design what product?

A. Ski parkas.

———◆———

Q. In 1642, Darby Field was the first European to climb what mountain?

A. Mount Washington.

Q. The summit of Mount Washington has how many overnight facilities?

A. None.

———◆———

Q. In Maine, what is the minimum age for a person to hunt when accompanied by an adult?

A. Ten years.

———◆———

Q. In Maine, what is the maximum number of dogs that can be used when hunting bears?

A. Four.

———◆———

Q. The hunting of what kind of deer is prohibited in New England?

A. Caribou.

———◆———

Q. In 1964, what Salem, New Hampshire, race track had the first legalized horse racing lottery since the Civil War?

A. Rockingham Park.

———◆———

Q. The Craftsbury Center in Craftsbury, Vermont, caters to devotees of what sport?

A. Sculling.

———◆———

Q. What state had the first ski touring center in America?

A. Vermont.

Q. In what baseball division does the Maine Phillies team play?

A. Triple A.

———————◆———————

Q. In what state is Mad River Glen?

A. Vermont.

———————◆———————

Q. What is the last town in which a northbound hiker on the Appalachian Trail can get supplies?

A. Monson, Maine.

———————◆———————

Q. What ski area in North Conway, New Hampshire, held the Volvo International Tournament?

A. Cranmore.

———————◆———————

Q. What group's motto reads: "To serve, to strive and not to yield"?

A. Outward Bound.

———————◆———————

Q. Mount Mansfield in Vermont is the home of what ski area?

A. Stowe.

———————◆———————

Q. At what Vermont ski area did Olympic gold medalist Andrea Mead Lawrence learn to ski?

A. Pico Peak.

Q. Is the tail of a snowshoe meant to be dragged or lifted?

A. Dragged.

———◆———

Q. What woman shared the 1984 Women's Sports Foundation Sportswoman of the Year title with Mary Lou Retton?

A. Joan Benoit.

———◆———

Q. In 1965, the smallest attendance at a world heavyweight title fight was recorded at Lewiston, Maine, at the bout between what two fighters?

A. Sonny Liston and Cassius Clay (Muhammed Ali).

———◆———

Q. Jordan Kobritz brought what professional sport to Maine?

A. Baseball.

———◆———

Q. For what sport is the Ellis River Trail in Jackson, New Hampshire, most commonly used?

A. Ski touring.

———◆———

Q. In what units are ski-touring distances measured at Bretton Woods?

A. Meters.

———◆———

Q. What kind of boat is most commonly used on the Allagash Waterway in Maine?

A. Canoe.

Q. The Mount Mansfield ski area is in what Vermont town?

A. Stowe.

———◆———

Q. What are the three basic types of snowshoes?

A. Maine (Michigan), Pickerel (Arctic or Alaska), and Bear Paw.

———◆———

Q. What canoes are known as "strippers"?

A. Cedar-strip canoes.

———◆———

Q. What New Hampshire native was the predecessor of coach Vincent Lombardi?

A. Ray ("Ramblin' Ray") McLean.

———◆———

Q. Where does the twenty-five-mile Newport, Vermont, Aquafest swim end?

A. Quebec.

———◆———

Q. Bill Dunlop sailed across what body of water in twenty-eight days?

A. The Atlantic Ocean.

———◆———

Q. In Vermont in 1934, what was powered by a Model-T engine, for the first time?

A. Rope tow for skiers.

Q. How many mountains are included in the Killington Ski Area?

A. Six.

———◆———

Q. What is free the first half-hour of operation every day at Mad River Glen?

A. Skiing.

———◆———

Q. What is the name of Vermont's only aerial tramway?

A. Jay Express.

———◆———

Q. The Maine Phillies is a farm team for what National League baseball team?

A. Philadelphia Phillies.

———◆———

Q. What type of winter sport trails link the inns in Franconia, New Hampshire?

A. Cross-country.

———◆———

Q. What is the name of the hut situated above the tree line on Mount Washington?

A. Lake of the Clouds.

———◆———

Q. Where is the headquarters of the Appalachian Mountain Club in New Hampshire?

A. Pinkham Notch.

Q. Moosehead Lake is an ideal environment for what three types of fish?

A. Brook trout, landlocked salmon, and togue.

———◆———

Q. What lake, east of Moosehead Lake, is sometimes called "the most natural trout factory"?

A. Sourdnahunk.

———◆———

Q. What are the four ski areas in the Mount Washington Valley?

A. Attitash, Wildcat, Cranmore, and Black.

———◆———

Q. What ski touring trail extends from northern to southern Vermont?

A. Catamount.

———◆———

Q. Who won North America's first World Cup Race at Cannon Mountain in 1967?

A. Jean-Claude Killy.

———◆———

Q. In the 1960 Winter Olympics, what New Hampshire skier won two silver medals?

A. Penny Pitou (of Laconia).

———◆———

Q. Where in the Wildcat ski area does the Wildcat Valley Trail begin?

A. At the top.

Q. What major July marathon is held in Bangor, Maine?

A. The Paul Bunyan Marathon.

Q. What mode of transportation takes skiers three and one-half miles up Killington Mountain ski area?

A. Gondola.

Q. The Outward Bound school in Maine is on what island?

A. Hurricane Island.

Q. What New England lake holds a fifty-mile water-ski marathon?

A. Lake Winnipesaukee (Laconia, New Hampshire).

Q. Where is the Head Classic Tennis Tournament held?

A. Stowe, Vermont.

Q. In Claremont, New Hampshire, the Over the River and Through the Wood relay races involve what three types of races?

A. Canoe, bicycle, and running.

Q. In Vermont, what is meant by a ski-touring trail sign showing a single, almost straight line?

A. An easy trail.

Q. What northern New England state has the most ski areas?

A. Vermont.

———◆———

Q. What trail is the Green Mountain Club responsible for maintaining?

A. The Long Trail.

———◆———

Q. The Goodrich map is published by an organization known by what acronym?

A. WVAIA (Waterville Valley Athletic and Improvement Association).

———◆———

Q. Where in Epping, New Hampshire, does motorcycle and drag racing take place?

A. New England Dragway.

———◆———

Q. What is the Alden Ocean Shell, manufactured in Eliot, Maine?

A. An open-water rowing boat.

———◆———

Q. What is the name of New England's first thoroughbred race track?

A. Rockingham Park.

———◆———

Q. On what mountain is the Greenleaf Hut?

A. Mount Lafayette.

Q. What is the current name of Belknap Mountain ski area?

A. Gunstock Mountain.

———◆———

Q. What Vermont native won the American medal for Olympic Nordic Skiing in 1976?

A. Bill Koch.

———◆———

Q. In order to use a snowmobile on the trails of Vermont, a traveler must be a member of what organization?

A. VAST (Vermont Association of Snow Travelers).

———◆———

Q. What type of oars are made by Dreissgacker Brothers in Morrisville, Vermont?

A. Sculling.

———◆———

Q. At age thirteen, golfing pro Patty Sheehan was rated the best in her age group at what sport?

A. Skiing.

———◆———

Q. What workers originally used the Avalanche Camp in the White Mountains, now a shelter for cross-country skiers?

A. Loggers.

———◆———

Q. What is the height of the vertical drop at Sugarloaf, the greatest in the East?

A. 2,637 feet.

Q. What five ski areas are part of "Ski 93" in New Hampshire?

A. Loon, Waterville Valley, Cannon, Mittersill, and Tenny.

Q. On what day does the Vermont Travel Division release the ski touring conditions for the weekend?

A. Thursday.

Q. What supermarket chain has used Robert Parish in its commercials?

A. Stop & Shop.

Q. What kind of vehicle was the *Rosie O'Grady*, which took Joe Kittinger from Maine to Italy?

A. A hot air balloon.

Q. What native New Hampshire wood is usually used to make snowshoes?

A. White ash.

Q. What is Nordic skiing?

A. Cross-country skiing.

Q. What competitive athlete consumes the most oxygen per minute?

A. A cross-country skier.

Q. For what wind would a sailor break out the spinnaker?

A. Downwind.

———◆———

Q. What kind of vessel is *The Fidelity,* which President George Bush keeps at his Maine summer home in Kennebunkport?

A. A power boat.

———◆———

Q. How many masts are there on each ship in the Maine Windjammer Association's fleet?

A. Two.

———◆———

Q. What kind of people can use the Pickerel or Alaska snowshoes to the best advantage?

A. Tall people.

———◆———

Q. What lake produced the world record landlocked salmon?

A. Sebago Lake.

———◆———

Q. What are the Yukon, the Modified Beaver Trail, and the Snowmobiler?

A. Snowshoes.

———◆———

Q. What do cross-country skiers call their high energy food that usually contains raisins, peanuts, and chocolate drops?

A. Gorp.

Q. How long was the Maine sailboat that broke the world's record crossing the Atlantic?

A. Nine feet.

Q. In how many of the northern New England states is the drinking age still eighteen?

A. None.

Q. What is the summit elevation at Sugarloaf/USA?

A. 4,237 feet.

Q. Sebago Lake is famous for what two kinds of fishing?

A. Trout and landlocked salmon.

Q. What is the only skiing area in Maine with views of Penobscot Bay?

A. Camden Snow Bowl.

Q. What is the most important game bird in New Hampshire?

A. Ruffed grouse.

Q. What two areas of New Hampshire are best for hunting woodcock?

A. Seacoast areas and northern counties.

Q. What are the two most important waterfowl species hunted in New Hampshire?

A. Black duck and wood duck.

◆

Q. What is the principal species of saltwater fish sought year round between Newburyport and Portsmouth, New Hampshire?

A. Striped bass.

◆

Q. What is the name of coastal Maine's oldest balloon voyage company, headquartered in Portland?

A. Balloon Sports.

◆

Q. In general, the upper Connecticut River is a better-than-average public stream for what fish?

A. Trout.

◆

Q. What is the most sought-after game fish on the Wild Ammonoosuc River?

A. Brook trout.

◆

Q. The Kancamagus Highway closely parallels what stream that is filled with brook and rainbow trout?

A. Swift River.

◆

Q. What New England state is reputed to have the best trout fishing in the Northeast because of its abundance of cold waters?

A. Vermont.

Q. What brook at Pittsford, Vermont, is one of the few eastern streams where rainbow trout have maintained themselves by natural spawning?

A. Furnace Brook.

———◆———

Q. Where is the Northeast's largest Aquaboggen water park?

A. Saco, Maine.

———◆———

Q. The Averill lakes, Lake Seymour, and Salem Lake in Vermont are the best waters in the state for what species of fish?

A. Landlocked salmon.

———◆———

Q. What warning does a lighted buoy on the ocean mean?

A. Underwater obstructions.

———◆———

Q. What two basic moves are involved in cross-country skiing?

A. The kick and the glide.

———◆———

Q. How many miles per day is considered average for a snowshoer in sound physical condition?

A. Eight to ten.

———◆———

Q. What animals race at the Seabrook, New Hampshire, race track?

A. Greyhound dogs.

Q. What New England ski area has the largest snowmaking system in the world?

A. Killington, Vermont.

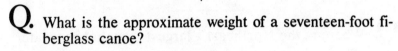

Q. What is the approximate weight of a seventeen-foot fiberglass canoe?

A. Between sixty-five and ninety-five pounds.

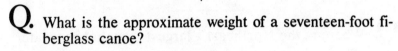

Q. In what city did the first international dog sled mail run arrive on January 14, 1929, after leaving Lewiston, Maine, on December 28, 1928?

A. Montreal, Canada.

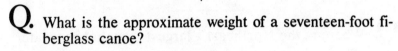

Q. What college did Joan Benoit attend?

A. Bowdoin.

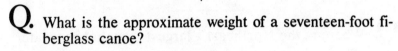

Q. Rectangular, barrel, and mummy are the three basic shapes of what L. L. Bean product?

A. Sleeping bags.

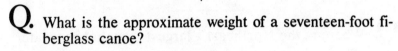

Q. Lightweight, three-season, and fixed-camp are the three basic categories of what camping item?

A. Tents.

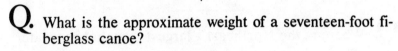

Q. What product can be put in an ice chest prior to storing to prevent musty odors?

A. Regular grind (not instant) coffee.

Q. How should the grain of an axe handle run at the knot end to reduce the chance of splitting?

A. Vertically.

———◆———

Q. For what type of fishing is Sebec Lake in Maine famous?

A. Landlocked salmon.

———◆———

Q. L. L. Bean suggested that a deer be dressed with what type of knife?

A. A jackknife.

———◆———

Q. By 1970, how many nonresidents had purchased deer hunting licenses in Maine?

A. Between 30,000 and 35,000.

———◆———

Q. What was the landing site of the first transatlantic hot air balloon, which left from Presque Isle, Maine?

A. Micrey, France.

———◆———

Q. Is Beechridge Speedway Maine's oldest, fastest, or largest stock car speedway?

A. Oldest.

———◆———

Q. As of 1989, how many times has Joan Benoit won the Boston Marathon?

A. Two.

Q. When sailing, what does it mean if a sailor is "reaching"?

A. The boat is sailing at a right angle to the wind.

———◆———

Q. In what recreational sport would one person say to another, "Track, please"?

A. Cross-country skiing.

———◆———

Q. What trail stretches 255 miles from Massachusetts to Canada through Vermont?

A. The Long Trail.

———◆———

Q. With forty-five miles of trail, fourteen lifts, and more than 400 acres of skiing, what is the largest ski area in Maine?

A. Sugarloaf.

———◆———

Q. What is the oldest mountaineering/conservation organization in the nation?

A. Appalachian Mountain Club.

———◆———

Q. How long are the pulling boats used on an Outward Bound sailing expedition?

A. Thirty feet.

———◆———

Q. A hiker on the Appalachian Trail must pitch camp a minimum of how many feet off the trail?

A. 200 feet.

SCIENCE & NATURE

C H A P T E R   F I V E

Q. What animal did the Algonquin name *musee,* which means "twig eater"?

A. The moose.

———◆———

Q. What is the minimum length of the antlers of a deer legally shot in the regular Vermont hunting season?

A. Three inches.

———◆———

Q. Camel's Hump is the third highest mountain in what state?

A. Vermont.

———◆———

Q. What 1947 disaster on Mount Desert Island in Bar Harbor, Maine, did an estimated thirty million dollars damage?

A. A forest fire.

———◆———

Q. "Mount Silversides" is the nickname for what Maine fish?

A. The landlocked salmon.

Q. Until 1868, New Hampshire was the sole U.S. commercial producer of what mineral?

A. Mica.

———◆———

Q. Which of the first seven astronauts lived in East Derry, New Hampshire?

A. Alan Shepard, Jr.

———◆———

Q. What is threatening the existence of the Prairie Fringed Orchid, found only in Maine?

A. Wildflower enthusiasts.

———◆———

Q. What can be seen at the Mount Desert Oceanarium?

A. The sea life of coastal Maine.

———◆———

Q. What kind of scallop is found most commonly along the coast of Maine?

A. Giant sea scallop.

———◆———

Q. From what does the name *Vermont* derive?

A. *Vert* and *Mont* (French for green mountain).

———◆———

Q. In what state was Hiram Stevens Maxim, who received his first patent for an improvement to the curling iron, born?

A. Maine.

Q. What Maine mountain has the largest deposit of felsitic rhyolite in the world?

A. Mount Kineo.

Q. What is the main occupation of those who live on Monhegan Island?

A. Fishing.

Q. What did John Deere of Rutland, Vermont, invent?

A. The steel plow.

Q. What did Chester Greenwood of Maine invent?

A. Earmuffs.

Q. What is the largest mammal living above the tree line on Mount Washington?

A. The weasel.

Q. What kind of deer are commonly found in Maine?

A. White-tailed deer.

Q. What two New England states have the longest common natural border?

A. Vermont and New Hampshire (along the Connecticut River).

Q. As a crow flies, Maine's coast is 230 miles long, but how long is the actual shoreline?

A. 3,500 miles.

◆

Q. The bullfrog is found throughout the United States except in what two areas?

A. Florida and northern Maine.

◆

Q. What months can coyote, woodchuck, porcupine, and red squirrels be hunted in Maine?

A. All twelve months.

◆

Q. What bait is traditionally used to lure Atlantic salmon in Maine?

A. Artificial flies.

◆

Q. How many black bears can a licensed hunter in Vermont shoot each year?

A. One.

◆

Q. What are the Cannon Balls, found in Franconia Notch, New Hampshire?

A. Mountain summits.

◆

Q. James Hartness of Springfield, Vermont, patented the sundial, but what optical invention made him famous?

A. The Turret Equatorial Telescope.

Q. What three animals are depicted on the Vermont Fish and Game Department's insignia?

A. Deer, trout, and grouse.

———◆———

Q. How old must a person be to get a New Hampshire fishing license?

A. Sixteen.

———◆———

Q. What northern New England state grows twelve percent of America's potatoes?

A. Maine.

———◆———

Q. What type of seal, found in Lake Champlain, likes fresh water?

A. The harbor seal.

———◆———

Q. What Maine river flows 140 miles from Moosehead Lake to the Atlantic?

A. Kennebec.

———◆———

Q. What New England states does Quebec's Mont Notre Dame region border?

A. Vermont, New Hampshire, and Maine.

———◆———

Q. What four states grow more potatoes than Maine?

A. Idaho, Washington, North Dakota, and Oregon.

Q. What type of water projects endanger the St. John River locoweed plant?

A. Hydroelectric.

———◆———

Q. What is the chief big game species found in Vermont?

A. The white-tailed deer.

———◆———

Q. What New Hampshire lake is considered the most productive landlocked salmon lake?

A. Lake Winnipesaukee.

———◆———

Q. What New England state has the fewest hazardous waste sites?

A. Vermont (two).

———◆———

Q. How long is the New Hampshire Atlantic coastline?

A. Eighteen miles.

———◆———

Q. What is the largest, most common heron in northern New England?

A. Great blue heron.

———◆———

Q. What New Hampshire mountain did the Indians call *Agiocochook?*

A. Mount Washington.

Q. Where are the trunks and main branches of dwarf willow trees, which are found on Mount Katahdin and in the White Mountains?

A. Underground.

———◆———

Q. Oats are grown mainly in what New England state?

A. Maine.

———◆———

Q. In what state is the Allagash River?

A. Maine.

———◆———

Q. What river bisects Manchester, New Hampshire?

A. The Merrimack.

———◆———

Q. How many deer can a hunter shoot per year in Maine?

A. One.

———◆———

Q. What are the two most common gulls in Maine and New Hampshire?

A. The herring and the great black-backed gulls.

———◆———

Q. What is the eider's favorite food?

A. Mussel.

Q. In the mouth of what river is the Portsmouth Naval Shipyard situated?

A. Piscataqua.

———◆———

Q. What is the name of the lake the Old Man of the Mountains looks over?

A. Profile.

———◆———

Q. What is the only place the Katahdin willow is found?

A. Mount Katahdin, Maine.

———◆———

Q. How many varieties of seafood can be found in the Gulf of Maine?

A. Thirty-two.

———◆———

Q. What color is a devil's paint brush, a flower found in Maine?

A. Orange-red and yellow.

———◆———

Q. What northern game bird is often called the "timber doodle"?

A. Woodcock.

———◆———

Q. How are New England bobcats usually caught?

A. By running them with dogs.

Q. What was the weight of the record landlocked salmon caught on Sebago Lake in 1907?

A. Twenty pounds, eight ounces.

———◆———

Q. In New Hampshire, what do the Sunapee trout, shortnose sturgeon, Indiana bat, and lynx have in common?

A. They are endangered species.

———◆———

Q. In 1934, the strongest winds ever measured on earth— 188 mph with one gust reaching 231 mph—were recorded on what mountain peak in New Hampshire?

A. Mount Washington.

———◆———

Q. What percentage of America's lobsters do Maine fishermen catch?

A. Seventy-five percent.

———◆———

Q. Where do Maine ospreys migrate in the winter?

A. South America.

———◆———

Q. What are *Suillus pictus,* which are abundant in New Hampshire, with some kinds being edible?

A. Mushrooms.

———◆———

Q. In February 1969, 97.8 inches of snow fell in five days on what New Hampshire mountain?

A. Mount Washington.

Q. Trap Day on Monhegan Island, Maine, is a New Year's Day celebration of the opening of what season?

A. Lobster

———◆———

Q. What tree received its name because it was discovered near Norway, Maine?

A. Norway pine

———◆———

Q. On what river can a hiker stand under Guillotine Rock or squeeze through the Lemon Squeezer?

A. Lost River.

———◆———

Q. During what two seasons can the snowshoe rabbit be hunted in Maine?

A. Fall and winter

———◆———

Q. What is the "queen" of Maine's saltwater fish?

A. Bluefin tuna.

———◆———

Q. The largest Vermont island is in what lake?

A. Lake Champlain.

———◆———

Q. What are Maine's two most valuable minerals?

A. Sand and gravel.

Q. What is the warmest month in northern New England?

A. July.

———◆———

Q. When was Maine's heaviest one-day rainfall recorded?

A. September 11, 1954 (during Hurricane Edna).

———◆———

Q. What type of fish is known as the "togue" in Maine?

A. Lake trout.

———◆———

Q. How high are the tides in Maine's Passamquoddy Bay, the highest in the United States?

A. Twenty to twenty-eight feet.

———◆———

Q. What state has marble quarries that are among the largest in the world?

A. Vermont.

———◆———

Q. Of the New England states, which has the highest percentage of federal land?

A. New Hampshire.

———◆———

Q. What group of eight small islands has their jurisdiction split between Maine and New Hampshire?

A. Isles of Shoals.

Q. What is the average wind speed on Mount Washington in New Hampshire?

A. Thirty-five miles per hour.

———◆———

Q. In Maine, what fish is called the "king of fresh water game fish"?

A. Atlantic salmon.

———◆———

Q. What type of trout, a world's record size, did Ernest Theoharis catch on Lake Sunapee in New Hampshire?

A. Sunapee.

———◆———

Q. What breed of horse was first developed in Vermont?

A. Morgan.

———◆———

Q. What New England state has the highest percentage of forested area in the United States?

A. Maine.

———◆———

Q. What world-record fish was caught near the Isles of Shoals, New Hampshire, in 1969?

A. An Atlantic cod (ninety-eight pounds, twelve ounces).

———◆———

Q. Vermont borders what 130-mile-long lake?

A. Lake Champlain.

Q. Of what type rock is the Old Man of the Mountains made?

A. Granite.

———◆———

Q. What type of fish was produced in the first federal fish hatchery in Bucksport, Maine?

A. Atlantic salmon.

———◆———

Q. On what Maine mountain is the Knife Edge Ridge located?

A. Mount Katahdin.

———◆———

Q. What is the largest fish found in Maine waters?

A. The bluefin tuna.

———◆———

Q. In what state is the endangered plant St. John Riverwood found?

A. Maine.

———◆———

Q. How many ledges combine to make the Old Man of the Mountains?

A. Three.

———◆———

Q. In the United States, nine-tenths of what type of insulation comes from the Hyde Park region of Vermont?

A. Asbestos.

Q. What is the most valuable softwood in Maine?

A. White pine.

———◆———

Q. In the papermaking process, what two softwoods are most often used in Maine?

A. Spruce and fir.

———◆———

Q. What is the largest lake in New Hampshire?

A. Lake Winnipesaukee.

———◆———

Q. What range of mountains extends the length of Vermont?

A. The Green Mountains.

———◆———

Q. Where are the largest granite quarries in the world?

A. Barre, Vermont.

———◆———

Q. How much of the peak of Mount Washington is granite?

A. None.

———◆———

Q. What New Hampshire site was named after the eighteenth-century settler Abel Crawford?

A. Crawford Notch.

Q. How many rivers and streams are there in Maine?

A. More than 5,000.

———◆———

Q. What New Hampshire mountain was named for Tom Crawford?

A. Mount Tom.

———◆———

Q. What New England state has the largest area covered by water?

A. Maine.

———◆———

Q. What is the highest peak in Vermont?

A. Mount Mansfield (4,393 feet).

———◆———

Q. Maine biologists are famous for their advanced techniques for rearing what kind of fish?

A. Salmon.

———◆———

Q. What is the largest lake entirely owned by Vermont?

A. Bomoseen Lake.

———◆———

Q. The peak of what mountain is the first part of the United States to catch the rays of the rising sun?

A. Mount Katahdin.

Q. In 1949, what kind of fish did Mrs. Earl Small catch on Maine's Messalonskee Lake, breaking the world record?

A. White perch.

———◆———

Q. What kind of fish are most abundant in Lake Champlain?

A. Perch.

———◆———

Q. What New York mountains can be seen from Burlington, Vermont?

A. The Adirondacks.

———◆———

Q. What is the Batten Kill, found in Arlington, Vermont?

A. A stream.

———◆———

Q. Who operates the Scarborough Marsh Nature Center, Maine's largest salt marsh?

A. Maine Audubon Society.

———◆———

Q. What large shrub with waxy flowers is rare in northern New England and is protected by law in Maine?

A. Rhododendron.

———◆———

Q. Vermont's Otter Creek drains into what body of water?

A. Lake Champlain.

Q. Approximately how many lakes and ponds are there in Maine?

A. 2,500.

———◆———

Q. What type of hare is usually found in the forests of northern Vermont?

A. Snowshoe hare.

———◆———

Q. What coastal New England state has the shortest Atlantic Coast line?

A. New Hampshire.

———◆———

Q. In October, Maine opens deer season to hunters, although restricting them to what weapons?

A. Bows and arrows.

———◆———

Q. In what state is Mooselookmeguntic Lake found?

A. Maine.

———◆———

Q. What is krummholz, encountered by hikers on Mount Washington?

A. Dense low mats of vegetation.

———◆———

Q. A lottery is held each year in Maine for one thousand licenses to hunt what animal?

A. Moose.

Q. What state has border jurisdiction of the Connecticut River?

A. New Hampshire.

———◆———

Q. What is the Maine state mineral?

A. Tourmaline.

———◆———

Q. What covers more than five-sixths of the state of Maine?

A. Forest.

———◆———

Q. The water supply for Portland, Maine, comes from what lake?

A. Sebago Lake.

———◆———

Q. What New England park is referred to as the park "where the mountains meet the sea"?

A. Acadia National Park.

———◆———

Q. Franconia State Park lies between the peaks of what two mountain ranges in New Hampshire?

A. Franconia and Kinsman.

———◆———

Q. What New England spring-fed lake has hundreds of islands and 183 miles of shoreline?

A. Lake Winnipesaukee.

Q. What is another name for a horse mackerel?

A. Bluefin tuna.

———◆———

Q. What is the land area of Maine?

A. 33,215 square miles.

———◆———

Q. What body of water contains Isle La Motte, South Hero Island, and North Hero Island?

A. Lake Champlain.

———◆———

Q. What is New Hampshire's largest, most active conservation organization?

A. The Audubon Society (more than 3,000 members).

———◆———

Q. Where is the only deep water harbor in New Hampshire?

A. Portsmouth.

———◆———

Q. What is the largest natural lake entirely in New England?

A. Moosehead.

———◆———

Q. What winter had the biggest recorded snowfall in Maine?

A. 1981–82 (158.8 inches).

Q. How many White Mountain ranger districts are there in Maine?

A. One.

———◆———

Q. Are blueberries in Maine usually "high-bush" or "low-bush"?

A. Low-bush.

———◆———

Q. What kind of trees cover most of Vermont's mountains?

A. Broadleaf deciduous trees.

———◆———

Q. What poisonous snakes can be found in the Moosehead Lake region?

A. None.

———◆———

Q. What is the most valuable hardwood in Maine?

A. Yellow birch.

———◆———

Q. What name is given to a lobster that weighs from one to one and one-fourth pounds?

A. Chicken lobster.

———◆———

Q. What was the first National Estuarine Reserve in northern New England?

A. Laudholm Farm.

Q. In Maine, a lobster can be trapped legally only if its carapace measures at least how many inches?

A. Five.

———◆———

Q. What is the third largest island in the continental United States?

A. Mount Desert Island.

———◆———

Q. Where are the biggest bluefish in the nation found?

A. Maine.

———◆———

Q. On what days of the week does Vermont permit hunting during season?

A. All days.

———◆———

Q. When does fishing season open on Lake Winnipesaukee?

A. April 1.

———◆———

Q. The St. John River is a boundary between what two political areas?

A. Maine and New Brunswick.

———◆———

Q. On Mount Washington, what saves early spring wildflowers from killing frost and winds?

A. A blanket of spring snow.

Q. What New England state has an upper size limit on lobster to be caught?

A. Maine.

Q. The only fjord on the east coast of the United States is in what town?

A. Somesville, Maine.

Q. How many islands make up the Calendar Islands in Casco Bay, Maine?

A. 365.

Q. What kind of animal was imported by Corbin Park in New Hampshire when it opened as a game preserve in the 1890s?

A. Wild boar.

Q. What type of rock is quarried in Proctor, Vermont?

A. Marble.

Q. What was used instead of a blueprint to facilitate early wooden shipbuilding in Maine?

A. A half-model.

Q. During what two months is the bull moose ill-tempered and often given to charging after people?

A. September and October.

Q. What state is America's largest natural blueberry grower?

A. Maine.

———◆———

Q. What is threatening Maine's spotted salamander?

A. Acid precipitation.

———◆———

Q. The New Hampshire porcupine is a member of what family?

A. Rodent.

———◆———

Q. Between what two parts of a lobster do Maine lobstermen measure to determine if it is legal size?

A. The eye socket and the base of the tail.

———◆———

Q. What color dye is produced by the bark of the American black oak tree found in northern New England?

A. Bright yellow.

———◆———

Q. During what season in Maine do the cones of an eastern hemlock tree mature?

A. Fall.

———◆———

Q. Apple cider can attain a maximum of what percent alcohol?

A. About eleven percent.

Q. What color do the leaves of the oak, sumac, and black cherry turn in the fall?

A. Crimson.

———◆———

Q. What is a skink, the only reptile of its kind to be found in northern New England?

A. A lizard.

———◆———

Q. What color dye can be produced from most flower petals, no matter what color they are?

A. Yellow.

———◆———

Q. How many bushels of apples are needed to make three gallons of cider?

A. One.

———◆———

Q. What is the Maine state tree?

A. White pine.

———◆———

Q. The eastern white pine turns orange after exposure to light, giving it what nickname?

A. Pumpkin pine.

———◆———

Q. How many needles are in each cluster of an eastern white pine tree?

A. Five.

Q. Why are spider crabs a nuisance to Maine lobstermen?

A. They eat bait.

———◆———

Q. What is a "brookie"?

A. A brook trout.

———◆———

Q. What Maine mammal is nicknamed "wingfooted"?

A. The seal.

———◆———

Q. About how many pounds of stocked fish can one acre of a northern New England lake support?

A. About three-fourths pound.

———◆———

Q. What color are the tentacles around the snout of the star-nosed mole, found all over New England?

A. Pink.

———◆———

Q. In what direction do the cones of a New Hampshire balsam fir tree grow?

A. Upright.

———◆———

Q. In lobstering jargon, what is a cull?

A. A one-clawed lobster.

Q. What are maidenhair, staghorn, spleewart, ostrich, and Christmas, all found in northern New England?

A. Ferns.

———◆———

Q. How many gallons of maple syrup will forty gallons of sap yield?

A. One.

———◆———

Q. What is the only northern New England mammal with a poisonous bite?

A. The short-tailed shrew.

———◆———

Q. What type of poisonous snake ranges from Texas and Oklahoma eastward, then into northern New England?

A. Copperhead.

———◆———

Q. How many grades of maple syrup are made throughout northern New England?

A. Four.

———◆———

Q. Harvested in Maine, lettuce laver and sea grass are also known as what tasty treat?

A. Sea lettuce.

———◆———

Q. When ice fishing, for what is an ice spud used?

A. To cut a hole in the ice.

Q. Found in northern New England, what is a *Gavia immer?*

A. A common loon.

———◆———

Q. What is the largest member of the deer family in northern New England?

A. Moose.

———◆———

Q. What is the smallest (three to four inches) mammal found in northern New England?

A. Thompson's pygmy shrew.

———◆———

Q. "Fry" and "fingerling" are names for the young of what type of animal?

A. Fish.

———◆———

Q. What is the "bell" on a moose?

A. Skin and hair that hangs from the throat.

———◆———

Q. What is the "tomalley," found in a lobster?

A. The liver.

———◆———

Q. What berry found in northern New England gives gin its flavor?

A. Juniper berry.

Q. What type of New Hampshire maple tree makes the best maple syrup?

A. Sugar maple or rock maple.

———◆———

Q. After apple cider has reached its maximum alcoholic content, what does it become?

A. Vinegar.

———◆———

Q. The ground hemlock found in northern New England produces a poisonous berry of what color?

A. Red.

———◆———

Q. What is the largest rodent in northern New England?

A. Beaver.

———◆———

Q. About how much does a black bear cub weigh at birth?

A. Nine ounces.

———◆———

Q. The inequiment is what part of a crustacean?

A. The shell.

———◆———

Q. How many surfaces are there on a needle of a northern New England Norway spruce tree?

A. Four.

Q. How often does the bull moose shed its antlers?

A. Yearly.

———◆———

Q. What is a parr, a smolt, or a grilse?

A. A young salmon.

———◆———

Q. What are Scandinavian lingonberries?

A. Mountain cranberries.

———◆———

Q. In what month does the bull moose shed its antlers?

A. January.

———◆———

Q. About how many gallons of sap does a mature Vermont maple tree produce in a good season?

A. Eight gallons.

———◆———

Q. Is the fancy grade of maple syrup light or dark amber?

A. Light amber.

———◆———

Q. What is the state flower of New Hampshire?

A. Purple lilac.

Q. What does maple sap taste and look like as it comes from the tree?

A. Water.

Q. What are the "belted Galloways," found at the Aldemere Farm in Rockport, Maine?

A. Cows.

Q. What lake bird is said to stay with the same mate for life?

A. Loon.

Q. What large shrub, the bud of which is Connecticut's state flower, is protected by Maine law?

A. Mountain laurel.

Q. Of what material were the original Indian canoes made?

A. Birch bark.

Q. What Vermont hare's coat changes from brown in the summer to white in the winter?

A. Snowshoe.

Q. What animal is called a "bruin" in New Hampshire?

A. A bear.

Q. What color are New Hampshire bunchberries?

A. Scarlet.

———◆———

Q. The northern New England Indians preferred what berries over blueberries?

A. Juneberries.

———◆———

Q. What is a *Homarus americanus*

A. A lobster.

———◆———

Q. What did the Indians in colonial northern New England use to sweeten their food?

A. Maple syrup.

———◆———

Q. What color are cones on a Maine balsam fir tree in June?

A. Purple.

———◆———

Q. What "electrical wizard" of Eliot, Maine, invented the trolley car and the fire alarm?

A. Moses Farmer.

———◆———

Q. What animals were imported to Maine from Newfoundland in 1986?

A. Caribous.

Q. What birds are called the "snowbirds" of northern New England?

A. Dark-eyed juncos.

———◆———

Q. What is a group of whales called?

A. A gam or a pod.

———◆———

Q. Of the eight families of salamanders found worldwide, how many can be found in northern New England?

A. Four.

———◆———

Q. What is the average lifespan of a moose?

A. Twelve years.

———◆———

Q. With what animal did colonial New Englanders confuse the moose?

A. The elk.

———◆———

Q. In July, bluefish migrate from the waters of what state to northern New England?

A. Florida.

———◆———

Q. How many segments make up the body of a lobster?

A. Twenty-one.

Q. Maine beaches are primarily eroded by winds from what direction?

A. Northeast.

———◆———

Q. What is a baby moose called?

A. A calf.

———◆———

Q. How many acres does Acadia National Park contain?

A. 32,000.

———◆———

Q. How many lobes are usually found on the leaf of a sugar maple tree?

A. Five.

———◆———

Q. Maine pumpkins grow poorly if planted next to what vegetable?

A. Potatoes.

———◆———

Q. In what season are sheep sheared in Vermont?

A. Spring.

———◆———

Q. What does "jacking a deer" mean?

A. Shining a light in its eyes to make the deer easy prey.

Q. What mountain range is the oldest in America?

A. The Appalachian.

———◆———

Q. What mammal, common in northern New England, is the only one that flies?

A. The bat.

———◆———

Q. How many islands are there off the coast of Maine?

A. More than 3,000.

———◆———

Q. What bird is sometimes called a "sea parrot" or a "flying cigar"?

A. A puffin.

———◆———

Q. What did the Stanley brothers of Maine invent?

A. The Stanley Steamer.

———◆———

Q. Because of the number of living creatures in the Gulf of Maine, the average underwater visibility is limited to how many feet?

A. Twenty.

———◆———

Q. About ninety percent of all sandworms and bloodworms sold to U.S. saltwater fishermen are produced in what state?

A. Maine.

Q. What is the state bird of Maine?

A. The chickadee.

———◆———

Q. What is the state flower of Maine?

A. The white pine cone and tassel.

———◆———

Q. Why does Maine have cooler weather than most of the rest of the United States?

A. Arctic air and coastal winds keep it from being warmed by the Gulf Stream air.

———◆———

Q. What adjective is often used to describe the coast of Maine?

A. "Rock-bound."

———◆———

Q. What is the state bird of New Hampshire?

A. The purple finch.

———◆———

Q. What are monadnocks, which New Hampshire mountains have five of?

A. Rock that did not wear down when all the land around it was eroded away.

Q. What is the state bird of Vermont?

A. The Hermit thrush.

———◆———

Q. What is the state flower of Vermont?

A. The red clover.

MISCELLANEOUS

C H A P T E R   S I X

Q. In what New England states can you find tax- and duty-free shops on the Canadian border?

A. Maine and Vermont.

———◆———

Q. Which northern New England turnpike has the greatest toll per mile?

A. The New Hampshire (sixteen miles, one dollar).

———◆———

Q. What state's insect is the honeybee?

A. Maine.

———◆———

Q. What was the name of Paul Bunyan's reversible dog?

A. Jacko.

———◆———

Q. What product did L. L. Bean first manufacture?

A. Bean boots (for hunters).

Q. Between what two locations was the first international telephone conversation held?

A. Calais, Maine, and New Brunswick, Canada.

———◆———

Q. What is the name of the monster reputed to live in Lake Champlain?

A. Champ.

———◆———

Q. What is Vermont's telephone area code?

A. 802.

———◆———

Q. In Maine, what kind of wood is chiefly used to make toothpicks?

A. Birch.

———◆———

Q. What Manchester, New Hampshire, company derived its name from the combination of the words *velvet* and *crochet?*

A. Velcro.

———◆———

Q. What is the state animal of Maine?

A. The moose.

———◆———

Q. What mountain is sometimes called Mount Misery?

A. Mount Washington.

Q. What New England state has the smallest black and Hispanic populations?

A. Vermont.

Q. For what harvest are children excused from school in Aroostook County, Maine?

A. Potato.

Q. Name the company in Peterborough, New Hampshire, that has tools and gadgets you never thought existed.

A. Brookstone Company.

Q. What does the North Star in the official state seal of Maine symbolize?

A. The northern location of Maine.

Q. How was Commodore Nutt of Manchester, New Hampshire, billed by P. T. Barnum?

A. As the smallest man in the world.

Q. What did Henry David Thoreau break at Tuckerman Ravine in the White Mountains?

A. His leg.

Q. What state ranks second (following Louisiana) in the nation in percentage of French-speaking people?

A. Maine.

Q. Which of the following is the farthest from Albany, New York, by road: Augusta, Maine; Provincetown, Massachusetts; or Montreal, Quebec?

A. Augusta, Maine.

———◆———

Q. Which of these terms is not a common nickname for a person from Maine: Mainiac, Mainian, Mainer, Downeaster?

A. Mainian.

———◆———

Q. In 1980, what New England state had the largest increase in population?

A. New Hampshire.

———◆———

Q. What ethnic heritage is celebrated during the Acadian Festival in Madawaska, Maine?

A. French.

———◆———

Q. In Berlin, New Hampshire, what device (named Big Bella) is used to locate missing persons in the woods?

A. A foghorn.

———◆———

Q. What was Maine's first television station?

A. WABI-TV (1953).

———◆———

Q. What New Hampshire commission created a souvenir whiskey bottle in honor of the Old Man of the Mountains?

A. The liquor commission.

Q. In Vermont, what kind of tax is levied on the rent of a lean-to at a campground?

A. Hotel tax.

———◆———

Q. What is New Hampshire's most popular beer in total sales?

A. Budweiser.

———◆———

Q. In what Maine town does George Bush own a home?

A. Kennebunkport.

———◆———

Q. What Vermont town has an Egyptian mummy buried in a cemetery?

A. Middlebury.

———◆———

Q. Who had a blue ox named Babe?

A. Paul Bunyan.

———◆———

Q. Companies of what type own ninety percent of the shore front on Moosehead Lake?

A. Paper companies.

———◆———

Q. What expression used by sailors is now the name of an organization where people learn about the wilderness?

A. Outward Bound.

Q. What is Vermont's oldest cheese factory?

A. Crowley Cheese Company.

———◆———

Q. What is the only state in the union to levy no personal income or general sales tax?

A. New Hampshire.

———◆———

Q. What is the minimum age at which a person can obtain a Maine driver's license, following completion of a driver's education course?

A. Fifteen.

———◆———

Q. What Maine festival uses a frying pan that is ten and one-half feet across, reputedly the largest in the world?

A. The Central Maine Egg Festival.

———◆———

Q. The king of New England periodicals, *Yankee Magazine*, also publishes a magazine about what state?

A. Alaska.

———◆———

Q. Winooski, the name of a town in northern Vermont, is an Indian word meaning what?

A. "Onion."

———◆———

Q. What state was almost named Laconia?

A. New Hampshire.

Q. What color tile is on the Mount Washington Hotel's roof?

A. Red.

———◆———

Q. What was the full name of the man who started the L. L. Bean company?

A. Leon Leonwood Bean.

———◆———

Q. Tom Hamilton of Sunapee, New Hampshire, plays bass for what rock and roll group?

A. Aerosmith.

———◆———

Q. What state was the first authorized to mint copper cents?

A. Vermont.

———◆———

Q. W. S. Wells and Sons in Wilton, Maine, is believed to be the only U.S. company that cans what product?

A. Dandelion greens.

———◆———

Q. According to L. L. Bean, what is the next most important part of a hunting outfit after the gun?

A. Footwear.

———◆———

Q. What two colors are Vermont's official state colors?

A. Green and gold.

Q. Weejuns are a product of what Maine Company?

A. Bass.

———◆———

Q. What was Ida M. Fuller's social security number?

A. 000-00-0001.

———◆———

Q. Elmer the Moose, who belonged to Paul Bunyan, was what kind of animal?

A. A dog.

———◆———

Q. Mrs. P. F. E. Albee of New Hampshire was the first door-to-door salesperson to be hired by what company?

A. Avon.

———◆———

Q. What hut in the White Mountains was first to be adapted for winter use?

A. Zealand Falls Hut.

———◆———

Q. What does Maine's motto "Dirigo" mean?

A. "I lead."

———◆———

Q. What drink did Dr. Thompson of Union, Maine, invent?

A. Moxie.

Q. Rudy Vallee, who grew up in Westbrook, Maine, and attended the University of Maine, starred in what 1961 Broadway hit?

A. *How to Succeed in Business Without Really Trying.*

Q. The Coolidge family in Vermont still owns what famous cheese factory?

A. Plymouth Cheese Company.

Q. What coastal town is the home of New Hampshire's first nuclear power plant?

A. Seabrook.

Q. What kind of water-dress did Leonard Norcross of Dixfield, Maine, invent in 1834?

A. A diving suit.

Q. What title did Carlene King Johnson of Vermont win in 1955?

A. Miss USA

Q. Maine passed a law in 1909 that forbade the export of what kind of power?

A. Hydroelectric.

Q. What nickname is written on Maine's automobile license plates?

A. Vacationland.

Q. Walker's Point in Maine was named after the maternal grandfather of what president?

A. George Bush.

———◆———

Q. What is the second largest commercial port in New England?

A. Portland, Maine.

———◆———

Q. In 1981, what New England ice cream did *Time* magazine vote "the best ice cream in the world"?

A. Ben and Jerry's.

———◆———

Q. Where is the eastern terminal of the Montreal pipeline?

A. Portland, Maine.

———◆———

Q. At forty-four gallons per person per year, New Hampshire ranks second in the country for consumption of what beverage?

A. Beer.

———◆———

Q. What New England state ranks forty-eighth in the nation in population?

A. Vermont (about 525,000 in 1983).

———◆———

Q. What are the call letters of the FM radio station in Portland on channel 101.9?

A. WPOR-FM.

Q. What building in Portland, Maine, hosts the event called the World's Largest Garage Sale?

A. Portland Civic Center.

———◆———

Q. How many submarines were launched on January 27, 1944, at the Portsmouth Naval Shipyard?

A. Four.

———◆———

Q. What is the symbol of the New Hampshire Audubon Society?

A. A loon.

———◆———

Q. What was Paul Bunyan's wife's name?

A. Minnie.

———◆———

Q. What Maine company is the world's largest paper manufacturer?

A. Scott Paper Company.

———◆———

Q. Stratham, New Hampshire, claims to be the only town in the world to have what?

A. The name Stratham.

———◆———

Q. What Manchester, New Hampshire, native started the boom in the fast food industry?

A. Dick McDonald.

Q. What New England state is the only one that does not require a blood test before marriage?

A. Maine.

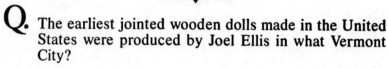

Q. The earliest jointed wooden dolls made in the United States were produced by Joel Ellis in what Vermont City?

A. Springfield.

Q. Besides in Maine, where is a University of New England located?

A. Armidale, New South Wales, Australia.

Q. What AM station has the call letters WRKD?

A. 1450 AM.

Q. In 1967, Vermont was the first state to outlaw what from the roadside?

A. Billboards.

Q. What New England state has had the least percentage of increase in population since 1790?

A. Vermont (600 percent).

Q. Several early transatlantic flights left from what very long, naturally hard-packed beach in Maine?

A. Old Orchard Beach.

Q. What is the New Hampshire telephone area code?

A. 603.

Q. What nickname has been given to Rochester, New Hampshire, because of the abundance of certain flowers?

A. "Lilac City."

Q. Bruce Johnson, a Bangor, Maine, resident, has taken what kind of act all over the country?

A. His magic act.

Q. What is an inhabitant of New Hampshire called?

A. A New Hampshirite.

Q. What is the New Hampshire state motto?

A. "Live Free or Die."

Q. What Wilton, Maine, shoe company has been making shoes for more than 105 years?

A. G. H. Bass and Company.

Q. What does *Ogunquit* mean in the Indian language?

A. "Beautiful place by the sea."

Q. What ships are overhauled at the Portsmouth Naval Shipyard?

A. Nuclear submarines.

———◆———

Q. Aroostook County, Maine, is the world's largest producer of what product?

A. Potatoes (and potato seeds).

———◆———

Q. What company produces Michelob and Budweiser beers?

A. Anheuser-Busch.

———◆———

Q. What kind of breaks at 11:00 A.M. and 4:00 P.M. did a Maine worker enjoy during the early 1800s?

A. Rum breaks.

———◆———

Q. What New England state does not restrict the pay-off for charity games?

A. Vermont.

———◆———

Q. What was State of Maine Spruce Gum?

A. Chewing gum.

———◆———

Q. Whose home is watched by "Bushwatchers"?

A. George Bush's.

Q. The Auto Museum in Wells, Maine, has examples of automobiles powered by what three different methods?

A. Steam, gasoline, and electricity.

———◆———

Q. What kind of store is Frisbee's, the oldest U.S. family-owned and family-run store of its type?

A. A grocery store.

———◆———

Q. In what state was the first paper mill established?

A. Maine.

———◆———

Q. In Maine, what kind of fish is traditionally served with egg sauce on July Fourth?

A. Salmon.

———◆———

Q. What northern New England state observes Patriots Day as a state holiday?

A. Maine.

———◆———

Q. How many cartons of American cigarettes can a non-Canadian resident bring into Canada without being taxed?

A. One.

———◆———

Q. What corn dish was developed Down East?

A. Creamed corn.

Q. What is hasty pudding?

A. Cornmeal mush.

———◆———

Q. What did northern New Englanders mean when they said someone "pegged out"?

A. The person died.

———◆———

Q. Where is the Maine Aquarium?

A. Saco.

———◆———

Q. In what city was Portsburger Lager beer once brewed?

A. Portsmouth, New Hampshire.

———◆———

Q. What FM radio station is the "voice of the mid-coast"?

A. Coast 102.5 FM.

———◆———

Q. How many feet from any residence must one be to discharge a firearm legally in Maine?

A. 100 feet.

———◆———

Q. What auto race track is in Oxford, Maine?

A. Oxford Plains Speedway.

Q. What magazine was first published in Camden, Maine, in 1924?

A. *Down East Magazine.*

———◆———

Q. What was the first radio station established in Maine?

A. WABI, Bangor.

———◆———

Q. With parental consent, what is the minimum age for a girl to marry in New Hampshire?

A. Thirteen.

———◆———

Q. What company can be called twenty-four hours a day, seven days a week to place a catalog order?

A. L. L. Bean.

———◆———

Q. What does the processing plant in Presque Isle—the largest of its type in the world—process?

A. Potatoes.

———◆———

Q. How many times a week is the *York County Coast Star* published?

A. Once.

———◆———

Q. What would Down Easters call a ruffed grouse?

A. A partridge.

Q. What is the minimum age for marriage in Maine?

A. Sixteen.

◆

Q. Where is the Maine State Music Theatre?

A. Bowdoin College Campus in Brunswick.

◆

Q. For what purpose did Maine sailors use dried pork tied to a string?

A. To ward off sea sickness.

◆

Q. What year was Maine's drinking age raised to twenty-one?

A. 1985.

◆

Q. What type of artist is Lorin Hollanden, who first appeared in concert at the Portland City Hall Auditorium in 1960?

A. Classical pianist.

◆

Q. What wild animal strolled around the Maine state capitol building a few years ago?

A. A moose.

◆

Q. Approximately how many islands are there in Lake Winnipesaukee, New Hampshire?

A. 300.

Q. Star Island is the largest of what group of islands?

A. Isles of Shoals.

———◆———

Q. What lighthouse in Maine is said to be the most photographed?

A. Nubble Lighthouse (York).

———◆———

Q. For how many regions of the United States does the *Old Farmer's Almanac* forecast the weather?

A. Sixteen.

———◆———

Q. In terms of area, about what percentage of New England is the state of Maine?

A. About fifty percent.

———◆———

Q. Where is the Shoals Marine Laboratory of the University of New Hampshire and Cornell University?

A. Isles of Shoals.

———◆———

Q. What New England state has the most miles of hiking trails?

A. Vermont.

———◆———

Q. How many national campgrounds are there in the Green Mountain National Forest?

A. Five.

Q. What city in New England is rated second largest of the oil ports on the east coast?

A. Portland, Maine.

Q. Approximately how many months each year is Moosehead Lake covered with ice?

A. Six.

Q. What is the 3,400-ton Green Mountain Giant in Vermont?

A. New England's largest boulder.

Q. At 33.69 inches, what state has the lowest average annual precipitation in New England?

A. Vermont.

Q. In what town did Andre the seal spend summers?

A. Rockport, Maine.

Q. The name of what New England lake means "the smile of the Great Spirit"?

A. Winnipesaukee.

Q. What cascade in the White Mountains was named after the Roman goddess of childbirth and forests?

A. Diana's Bath.

Q. What state holds the lowest statewide temperature record in New England at −50°F?

A. Vermont.

———◆———

Q. With a population of 2,300, what is the smallest incorporated city in the United States?

A. Vergennes, Vermont (incorporated in 1788).

———◆———

Q. The town of Wilson Mills, Maine, spent $2,500 one winter to feed what kind of animals?

A. Deer.

———◆———

Q. The forty-fifth degree latitude is the approximate northern border for what New England state?

A. Vermont.

———◆———

Q. How old must a maple tree be before it is worth tapping for sap?

A. About forty years.

———◆———

Q. How many people were killed by the 1938 hurricane in New England (names had not yet been assigned to hurricanes)?

A. 600.

———◆———

Q. What is described by the terms *head, kitchen, shark's mouth,* and *parlor?*

A. Lobster trap.

Q. Where was the center of the 5.2 magnitude earthquake that shook New England on October 7, 1983?

A. The Adirondack Mountains, New York.

———◆———

Q. In the western mountains of Maine, what does finding "color" in a pan mean?

A. Finding gold.

———◆———

Q. In Maine, what kind of wood is considered the "warmest" wood?

A. White cedar.

———◆———

Q. What two northern New England states currently have the death penalty?

A. Vermont and New Hampshire.

———◆———

Q. In New Hampshire, a straw skep was the traditional symbol of what profession?

A. Beekeeping.

———◆———

Q. From where did the marble headstone on John F. Kennedy's gravesite come?

A. A Danby, Vermont, quarry.

———◆———

Q. How many calories are in one pound of Maine shrimp tails?

A. 400 to 500.

Q. According to Yankee weather superstitions, what can be expected when pine needles hang together and are dark in color?

A. A storm.

———◆———

Q. What was the profession of the New Englander who invented the slicker raincoat over 200 years ago?

A. Fisherman.

———◆———

Q. What is the Maine state fish?

A. Landlocked salmon.

———◆———

Q. How many pounds of lobster were harvested in Maine in 1985?

A. Over 20.1 million.

———◆———

Q. Where is the Thunder Hole (roaring waves pouring through a narrow chasm into a small cavern)?

A. Acadia National Park.

———◆———

Q. What is the earliest recorded frost date in Maine?

A. September 5 (1963).

———◆———

Q. Jill Ireland, Windsor, Vermont, resident and screen actress, was born in what country?

A. England.

Q. Where is statesman Edmund Muskie's family home?

A. Kennebunk Beach, Maine.

Q. What were the only two New England states that did not experience bank closure during the Great Depression?

A. Vermont and Rhode Island.

Q. Of the forty-eight contiguous states, which was never visited by Harry Truman during his campaigns?

A. Vermont.

Q. What was the profession of Samuel Hopkins, who was granted the first U.S. patent?

A. Potash maker.

Q. What percentage of Vermont's population is Roman Catholic?

A. About 30 percent.

Q. Springfield, Vermont, has been described as a heavy manufacturing center completely surrounded by what?

A. Cows.

Q. Where does the Camden Shakespeare Company perform?

A. Camden Amphitheatre, Maine.

Q. How many children did Isaiah Tolman, the first European to settle in Rockland, Maine, have?

A. Twenty-one.

———◆———

Q. Where is New England's only cement plant?

A. Thomaston, Maine.

———◆———

Q. What is the name of the speedway in Epping, New Hampshire?

A. Star Speedway.

———◆———

Q. Where is New England's largest "waterpark"?

A. Water Country in Portsmouth, New Hampshire.

———◆———

Q. What was the population of the Vermont Grants in 1777?

A. 25,000.

———◆———

Q. Where is Maine's oldest restored cruise boat still in operation?

A. Moosehead Lake.

———◆———

Q. Lake Champlain Chocolates is best known for what product?

A. Black and white chocolate Holstein cows.

Q. What restaurant in Dover Point, New Hampshire, serves the most seafood in the state?

A. Newicks.

Q. What was the original use of the building where the University of New Hampshire's Dairy Bar is located?

A. Railroad station.

Q. Where is the best place to get turkey in Meredith, New Hampshire?

A. Hart's Turkey Farm.

Q. What is New Hampshire's northernmost and smallest notch?

A. Dixville Notch.

Q. What are the three main pastimes in the Mount Washington Valley?

A. Hiking, skiing, and shopping.

Q. Where is Story Land, a paradise for young children?

A. Glen, New Hampshire.

Q. What New Hampshire town is home to Santa's Village and Six Gun City?

A. Jefferson.

Q. What ores were mined at Ruggles Mine in Grafton, New Hampshire?

A. Mica, feldspar, and beryl.

———◆———

Q. What does the Algonquin name *Sunapee* mean?

A. "Goose Lake."

———◆———

Q. Who shows up at the annual Rock Festival in Gilsum, New Hampshire?

A. People who buy, sell, and trade rocks.

———◆———

Q. Where is the New Hampshire Winery situated?

A. Laconia.

———◆———

Q. How long does it take to reach the top of Mount Washington by rail?

A. More than an hour.

———◆———

Q. What is the Castle in the Clouds?

A. An old summer mansion in Moultonborough, New Hampshire.

———◆———

Q. What town was the site of Daniel Webster's first murder trial?

A. Plymouth, New Hampshire.

Q. For what kind of trophies is the Morse Museum in Warren, New Hampshire, well known?

A. Big game.

◆

Q. Where does the Winnipesaukee Railroad travel?

A. Meredith to Weirs Beach, New Hampshire.

◆

Q. What is the oldest summer resort in the United States?

A. Wolfeboro, New Hampshire.

◆

Q. What is the stream running through Amherst, New Hampshire?

A. Quoquinnapassakessannagnog.

◆

Q. Merrimack was the home of what Indian tribe?

A. Penacook.

◆

Q. In what Maine town is Caterpillar Hill?

A. Sedgwick.

◆

Q. For whom was Ellsworth, Maine, named?

A. Former U.S. Supreme Court Chief Justice Oliver Ellsworth.

Q. Where in Maine is the "Grand Canyon of the East"?

A. Brownville Junction.

———◆———

Q. What fish are canned in Milbridge, Maine?

A. Sardines.

———◆———

Q. Instead of donkeys, what kind of animal is frequently used to haul gear on mountain treks in Maine?

A. Llamas.

———◆———

Q. What does the Indian word *Skowhegan* mean?

A. "A place to watch for fish."

———◆———

Q. What state in the Union has the lowest percentage of city dwellers?

A. Vermont.

———◆———

Q. What form of government, called the purest type of democracy, is used by northern New England towns?

A. The town meeting.

———◆———

Q. In 1823, what pioneer educator established the first teacher training school in the United States in Concord, Vermont?

A. Samuel Read Hall.

Q. How was Maine's admission to the Union involved in the Missouri Compromise?

A. Maine entered as a free state, Missouri as a slave state, to keep the numbers balanced.

———◆———

Q. What is Maine's time zone?

A. Eastern.

———◆———

Q. What nationally known event takes place each February in Hanover, New Hampshire?

A. Dartmouth College's Winter Carnival.

———◆———

Q. Why is the fourth Monday in April a statewide legal holiday in New Hampshire?

A. It is Fast Day, honoring provincial governor John Cutt.

———◆———

Q. The New Hampshire Music Festival is held in July and August in what three towns?

A. Gilford, Meredith, and Plymouth.

———◆———

Q. Why do tourists from all over the country converge on Vermont in September and October?

A. To see the autumn leaves.

———◆———

Q. What do visitors to Millstone Hill in Barre, Vermont, enjoy watching?

A. Large granite blocks being quarried, sawed, polished, and carved.

Q. What Bellows Falls, Vermont, museum houses the Union Pacific "Big Boy," the largest steam locomotive ever built?

A. The Steamtown Foundation for the Preservation of Steam and Railroad Americana, Inc.

———◆———

Q. Fort Constitution in New Castle, New Hampshire, was originally named for what English monarchs?

A. William and Mary.

———◆———

Q. What was the first proprietary degree-granting medical college in the country?

A. Castleton Medical College, Vermont (1821).

———◆———

Q. In what year was the 400-acre MacDowell Colony for artists established in Peterborough, New Hampshire?

A. 1907.

———◆———

Q. In 1920, what poet purchased Sharftsbury, Vermont's "half-stone house," which has stone walls twenty-two inches thick?

A. Robert Frost.

———◆———

Q. What Maine island did Admiral Robert E. Peary name for the whaling ship that first took him to the Arctic?

A. Eagle Island.

———◆———

Q. How many sides does Richmond, Vermont's Round Church, actually have?

A. Sixteen.

Q. What Kennebunkport, Maine, museum is said to have one of the most comprehensive collections of electric street cars in the world?

A. The Seashore Trolley Museum.

———◆———

Q. In what picturesque area of Lake Champlain did Ethan Allen muster his Green Mountain Boys prior to the 1775 assault on Fort Ticonderoga?

A. Hand's Cove.

———◆———

Q. When was Augusta, Maine's Blaine House first used as the official residence of the governor?

A. 1919.

———◆———

Q. The *Seguin,* the oldest U.S. registered wooden steam tug (1884), is berthed at what historic Bath, Maine, shipyard?

A. Percy and Small Shipyard.

———◆———

Q. Whose patronage of Vermont's Black River Academy (1888) and Ludlow Graded School (1871–72) made the survival of those two historic sites possible?

A. Calvin Coolidge.

———◆———

Q. What Bethel, Maine, artist and inventor founded *Scientific American?*

A. Rufus Porter.

———◆———

Q. What Montpelier, Vermont, native founded National Life Insurance Company?

A. Dr. Julius Dewey.

Q. What noted humanitarian designed the organ in the Lorimer Chapel of Colby College, Waterville, Maine?

A. Albert Schweitzer.

———◆———

Q. Where is the birthplace of George Perkins Marsh, who laid the philosophical foundations of America's conservation movement?

A. Woodstock, Vermont.

———◆———

Q. What Wiscasset, Maine, landmark has a collection of more than one thousand music boxes?

A. Musical Wonder House (1852).

———◆———

Q. What Derby Line, Vermont, landmark was built half in Canada and half in the United States?

A. The Haskell Free Library and Opera House (1901–04).

———◆———

Q. Clara H. Nash, the first woman to be admitted to the bar in New England, practiced law in what Maine town?

A. Machias.

———◆———

Q. In 1843, who discovered iron ore on Maine's Ore Mountain?

A. Moses Greanleaf.

———◆———

Q. On what Maine lake is the Lakewood Theater, reputedly the oldest summer theater in America?

A. Lake Wesserunsett.

Q. What three Maine villages make up the York historical district?

A. York Harbor, York Corner, and York Village.

———◆———

Q. "A sapphire close against the sky" was Nathaniel Hawthorne's description of what New Hampshire mountain?

A. Monadnock.

———◆———

Q. What Dublin, New Hampshire, artist was well known for his series of mother-and-child portraits?

A. George de Forest Brush.

———◆———

Q. What New Hampshire town was the birthplace of the Pillsbury brothers, founders of the nation's largest flour business?

A. South Sutton.

———◆———

Q. The waters of what New Hampshire spa and resort were once called "baby waters" because of the number of large families in the area?

A. Clarendon Springs.

———◆———

Q. The area around what New Hampshire town was the setting for *Coniston*, Winston Churchill's political novel?

A. Cornish.

———◆———

Q. What Maine town was named for an English cathedral town?

A. Wells.

Q. Meriden, New Hampshire's nickname of "Bird Village" is the result of the activities of what noted naturalist?

A. Ernest Harold Baynes.

———◆———

Q. During the early 1900s, what settler became the well-known guardian of the road through Sandwich Notch?

A. Moses Hall.

———◆———

Q. The name of what Maine area is a word that means "meeting place of the alewives"?

A. Damariscotta.

———◆———

Q. According to local legend, what rocky hillside near Bristol, Vermont, contains a fortune in buried treasure?

A. Hell's Half Acre.

———◆———

Q. What Maine city calls itself "The Boating Capital of New England"?

A. Boothbay Harbor.

———◆———

Q. What shy Jericho, Vermont, photographer made over 5,000 photographs of individual snowflakes?

A. W. A. Bentley.

———◆———

Q. In 1832, the area around Pittsburg, New Hampshire, declared itself to be independent of either the United States or Canada, adopting what name?

A. The Republic of Indian Stream.

Q. On what Maine island are there strange rock inscriptions thought to be "Viking grafitti" by many historians?

A. Manana.

———◆———

Q. The Electrolytic Marine Salts Company, founded in 1896 in North Lubec, Maine, claimed to be able to extract what substance from seawater?

A. Gold.

———◆———

Q. What eighteenth-century pirate, nicknamed "Robin Hood of the High Seas," chose Maine's Machias region as a retirement base, only to drown with his crew as his ship foundered on the rocks?

A. Samuel Bellamy.

———◆———

Q. What was the name of the first schooner built in Camden, Maine, launched in 1769?

A. *George C. Wells*.

———◆———

Q. What Woodford, Vermont, native founded the Western Cartridge Company, which eventually took over the historic Winchester Repeating Arms Company?

A. Franklin W. Olin.